A NOTE-BOOK OF
MEDIAEVAL HISTORY

A NOTE-BOOK OF
MEDIAEVAL HISTORY

A.D. 323—A.D. 1453

BY

CHARLES RAYMOND BEAZLEY

BOOKS FOR LIBRARIES PRESS
FREEPORT, NEW YORK

First Published 1917
Reprinted 1971

INTERNATIONAL STANDARD BOOK NUMBER:
0-8369-5824-1

LIBRARY OF CONGRESS CATALOG CARD NUMBER:
70-160957

PRINTED IN THE UNITED STATES OF AMERICA

PREFATORY NOTE

THIS Note-book is an attempt to arrange the chief lines in the European history of the Middle Ages: (1) according to order of time; (2) without division by countries, or by any other method except the chronological; (3) in comparatively short periods; (4) with inclusion of fairly copious reference to the history of culture and civilization as well as to that of politics. Under *Civilization* I try to give some notes on the history of European Literature, Commerce and Industry, Discovery and Invention, Science and Art, Philosophy and Religion. The history of the Church especially—Eastern and Western—has been treated with an endeavour to recognize its unique importance during most of this time—from the fourth to the fifteenth century of Christ.

In many ways the Middle Ages bear more directly on our present life and problems—our trivial lives and fortunes in the twentieth century—than more 'modern' times. Especially is this apparent from the study of nationalism. This is the force which dominates the politics, and sometimes devastates the countries, of the present day; the same force creates the modern nations in the Middle Ages. The volcano never really sleeps; but its energies, in some respects, are perhaps

less fierce in the times and through the action of the
Classical Renaissance and the Protestant Revolution.
Both Germany and France may, perhaps, be thought
to bear some witness in this case.

I owe thanks especially to the suggestions of Professor
Tout and Professor Tait, of Manchester, and to Miss
C. Vaudrey for valuable clerical help.

C. R. B.

January 1917.

CONTENTS

CONTENTS

PERIOD I

FROM THE ADOPTION OF CHRISTIANITY BY THE ROMAN STATE TO THE BEGINNING OF THE PERMANENT BARBARIAN INVASIONS AND SETTLEMENTS ('VÖLKERWANDERUNG'), 323-75 A.D.

GENERAL POINTS

1. The Roman **Empire** remains practically **intact** throughout this period. The civilization, power, and territory of the Helleno-Roman World are only changed in religion. Otherwise 'ancient conditions' continue. But a **new**, Oriental, **capital (Constantinople)** is given to the Empire.

2. The **adoption of Christianity** by the State and governing classes, which is the first important step from the Ancient World to the Mediaeval (and Modern), is the supreme feature of this time. Julian's attempt at a Pagan restoration is a failure. The 'Orthodox' and 'Catholic' Church, organized as the established Church of the Empire (a new thing), holds its first 'General Council', in which the belief of the Christian community is defined.

3. The great movement of the Barbarian peoples into the Roman World—the **Wandering of the Nations**—begins at the end of this period, but really belongs to the next.

323   **Constantine** the Great (joint-emperor from 306, sole emperor 323–37) *becomes a* **Christian** *catechumen* ; he is only baptized on his death-bed. In large measure he *recognizes Christianity as the* most favoured *State religion*. Yet he abstains from open war against Pagan cults as a whole, professing indeed a wish to reform them. His court remains largely, his bureaucracy almost wholly, Pagan. But he forbids the State sacrifices of Paganism, and the occult and openly immoral parts of Pagan worship (witchcraft, divination, ' evil magic ', ' lying oracles ', and the religious orgies of certain Oriental rites and their imitators in the West). This involves the neglect and disfavour of Pagan beliefs and cults, as Christianity will not, like other creeds of the Graeco-Roman World, take the position of one among many.

' The Christianity of Constantine must be allowed in a more . . . vague and qualified sense [than often asserted] : the nicest accuracy is required in tracing the . . . gradations by which the monarch declared himself the Protector, and at length the Proselyte, of the Church ' [Gibbon, ch. xx].

Probably Constantine admitted Christianity as ' *a* true religion' (i.e. as a faith, at any rate, beneficial and ennobling to Man and the State) long before he granted its claim to be the only true religion.

' During his reign the stream of Christianity flowed with a gentle, though accelerated, motion ' [Gibbon, ch. xx].

324, &c.   (First) Church of St. John Lateran, Rome (the proper Cathedral of the Popes), built by Constantine.

c. 325–
336, &c.   Churches and other buildings of the Emperor Constantine and his mother Helena at Jerusalem and Bethlehem (' the Holy Sepulchre ', ' the Nativity ', &c.).

The fable of ' Constantine's Donation ', supported by forgeries of the eighth and ninth centuries [see 772, 860], associated Constantine's ' establishment ' of the Catholic

Church with a supposed endowment. Constantine ' with-
drew from the . . . patrimony of St. Peter . . . founding
a new capital in the East ; and resigned to the Popes the
free and perpetual sovereignty of Rome, Italy, and . . . the
West ' [Gibbon, ch. xlix]. So Dante :

> ' Ah, Constantine—of how much ill was mother,
> Not thy conversion, but that marriage-dower,
> Which the first wealthy Father took from thee.'
>
> [*Inferno*, xix.]

Council of Nicaea.   *The* **First General** (' *Oecumenical* ') **325**
Council *of the Christian Church* meets under the protection
of the emperor, at Nicaea (Nikaia) in Bithynia, close to
the city already selected for the new imperial capital
(Byzantium).

This Council *condemns Arianism* (the doctrine of Areios
or Arius of Alexandria, which did not recognize the absolute
Godhead of Christ), and *asserts the ' Athanasian ' and
' Catholic ' belief*, championed by **Athanasius,** Bishop of
Alexandria (296–373).

This is the most important of the early doctrinal struggles
of Christianity, and the subsequent development of both
the Roman and Greek portions of the Church largely
depends on it.

The greater part of the *Nicene Creed*, in which the
divinity of Christ is elaborately stated (. . . ' Very God of
Very God, Begotten not Made, being of One Substance
with the Father ' . . .), is also issued in its first form by
this Council (completed by Council of Constantinople, 381).

Development of Christian pilgrimage. (' Bordeaux pil-
grim ' to Jerusalem, 333—the first important record of
Christian pilgrim-travel.)

Old St. Peter's, Rome, ' which for size has no equal in **326, &c.**
the world ', the principal church of Western Christendom,
built by Constantine. (It is demolished and rebuilt as the
present St. Peter's in the fifteenth and sixteenth centuries.)

330 *Byzantium chosen by Constantine as the* **New Capital** *of the Empire* ; its name is to be changed to ' New (or Second) Rome ', *Nova Roma* ; but the popular tendency conquers, and the new capital becomes the ' City of Constantine ', **Constantinopolis.** The planting of the court at Constantinople completes a transition which has long been at work (*int. al.*, through dislike of recent emperors to Rome itself). Diocletian (284–305) had fixed his seat at Nicomedia (Nikomedeia) in NW. Asia Minor, while his nominal Colleague and real Viceroy, Maximian, though living in Italy, had neglected Rome, and resided at Milan.

Even after 395 Western Emperors reside not at Rome, but at Ravenna, like the ' exarchs ' after 560 (see p. 29).

Imperial Constantinople, immensely enlarged from old Byzantium (perhaps ten times larger under Constantine, still further increased in the next century), is soon equal to Rome in population, and superior in wealth ; as a first-class harbour it develops a great trade. *From the fifth century* (if not from the fourth) *to the beginning of the thirteenth it is certainly the largest, richest, and most luxurious city of the Christian world.* From its refoundation it is, moreover, a Christian city, and for a time the political capital of Christendom. But it never succeeds in becoming the spiritual capital.

The Bishops of Constantinople rank, from this time, among the chiefs of the Christian hierarchy (' Patriarchs '), but the *vague primacy already accorded to the Bishops of Rome* becomes more and more definitely asserted and admitted, and is gradually transformed into a complete supremacy over the greater part of Christendom [all the West].

The history of Christian Constantinople (330–1453) is curiously coincident with the mediaeval period as a whole.

c. 330– *Beginnings of Christian monastic communities* in Egypt **340** (solitary monasticism goes back much earlier—in Egypt at least to about A.D. 250).

Constantine reorganizes the Empire somewhat after the **c. 33 ?-** Diocletian manner (four prefectures—the East, Illyricum, **37** Italy, Gaul ; subdivided into civil dioceses and provinces). He also carries on the tendency towards an Oriental despotic court, with elaborate ceremonial, and remodels the taxation. He maintains peace and order throughout the Roman World, and secures the safety of the Empire against foreign enemies.

At the end of his life he *makes full profession of Chris-* **337** *tianity* (see above, 323), and divides the Empire, again imitating Diocletian, among his three sons as joint *Augusti*, with two nephews as *Caesars*. This system, which had worked well under Diocletian, is a failure in the family of Constantine, 337-50.

Death of Eusebius, ' father of Church history ' (born **340** about 267 ; Bishop of Caesarea in Palestine, 313 ; friend and confidant of Constantine the Great, who put him on his right hand at the Council of Nicaea). His *Ecclesiastical History*, the earliest important work of its kind, is of high value.

Progress of Christianity among the Teutonic tribes border- **c. 348** ing the Empire. ' Ulfilas ' (Wulfila), ' apostle ' and bishop of the Goths (b. 311), heads a *settlement of Gothic Christians within the Empire*—in the later Bulgaria, 348 [see also 375]. *Ulfilas's translation of the Bible* (minus *Samuel, Kings,* and *Chronicles,* books dangerously stimulating to a warlike people), the oldest monument of Teutonic speech.

After thirteen years of unsatisfactory division, civil war, **350** and general weakening of the Empire, Constantius, the second son of Constantine, reunites the Empire. He appoints his cousin Julian, ' the Apostate ', as Viceroy (' Caesar ') in Gaul, 356.

Death of Antony ' of the Thebaid ', the chief leader of **356** the new Christian monasticism, in its first home, Egypt.

This movement had spread to Rome by 341 ; thence, in modified forms, it reaches other countries of the West. But the true western monasticism begins in the sixth century, with St. Benedict [see below, p. 33].

Jealous of Julian's successes in government and war (victories over Alamanni at Strassburg, 357, &c.), Constantius attempts to weaken his army, and thus provokes a fresh civil war. At the beginning of this, Constantius dies, and Julian becomes sole emperor.

361-3   Reign of Julian. Hating Christianity (which he had professed up to the war with Constantius, and then repudiated : hence the title of ' Apostate ', *Apostata*, applied to him by Catholic writers), he is devoted to Greek philosophy, and makes the **restoration of Paganism**, *in a philosophical and purified form*, the principal object of his reign.

Project to rebuild the Temple of Jerusalem.

Julian's expedition against the Persians, at first successful, ends in failure and in the death of the emperor (' Vicisti Galilaee ' legend).

363-4   His successor, the Christian Jovian, to save the army which had elected him, concludes an ignominious peace with Persia, ceding the provinces beyond the Tigris, with part of Mesopotamia, and abandoning the Roman supremacy over Armenia.

363   **Christianity restored** *as an official and privileged faith of the Empire. Steady decline of Paganism*, no revival of which is seriously undertaken after Julian's death.

364   Valentinian, elected emperor by the army after the death of Jovian, appoints his brother Valens as co-emperor in the East.

373   Death of St. Athanasius (b. 296; Bishop of Alexandria, 326-73), the leading champion of the doctrine of the divinity of Christ against Arius and Arianism. The victory of Athanasius marks an epoch in the history of Christianity.

PERIOD II

FROM THE BEGINNING OF THE PERMANENT BARBARIAN INVASIONS ('VÖLKERWANDERUNG') TO THE CAPTURE OF ROME BY THE GOTHS, 375–410

GENERAL POINTS

1. The first important stages of the great migrations—'**the Wandering of the Nations**'—fall within these years. Germanic (with Slavonic and other) races press into the Empire, capture Rome itself, and begin to beat down resistance in the west of Europe.

2. **The old civilization** in great part begins to **crumble away,** certain elements being protected by the Church, which to some extent prevents a complete relapse into barbarism. The Germanic and other conquerors gradually learn to value the tradition of Greece and Rome.

3. The **increasing power** and the **civilizing spirit** of the **Christian Church** are shown in this time (still more later), in the Church's dealings both with the northern conquerors and with the Old Empire, under the last emperor of the whole Roman World, Theodosius I.

4. The **fall** of the old Helleno-Roman **Paganism** is outwardly complete by about 400 in the chief centres of population.

Under Augustus fails the only serious Roman attempt at the conquest of the German peoples. From the end of the second century A.D., Germanic attacks dangerously trouble the Roman frontiers. In the middle of the third century, during the first period of Roman decline and disintegration (the so-called 'Thirty Tyrants of Rome', &c.), Goths and others break through the frontier defences, and the fall of the Empire seems at hand. But by the imperial restoration of Aurelian and his successors the dissolution of the Roman World is deferred for over a century. Now the time of dissolution approaches for the West.

The storm, however, breaks in the East.

c. 375   At this time the East Goths are chiefly settled on the north and north-west of the Black Sea, up to the Roman (Danube) frontier ; the West Goths in (modern) South Rumania and East Hungary (formerly the Roman Dacia—till about A.D. 180 the Goths are mainly to be found in the basin of the Vistula) ;—the Vandals are in West Hungary ; the Franks on the Lower Rhine ; the Lombards on the Lower Elbe ; the Saxons between Elbe and Rhine. A part of the Gothic race, converted to Arian Christianity by Wulfila ('Ulfilas') in the early and mid fourth century, have settled within the Empire south of the Lower Danube, 348, &c. [see above].

Pressed by attacks from other races on the side of Asia (Huns crossing the Volga, Alans, &c.), the East and West Goths move forward to the south and west ; many more of the *Christian Goths* (mainly West-Gothic) are *allowed to pass into the Empire*, where they join their fellow countrymen south of the Danube, 375 [see also 348].

Meantime, beyond the Danube, the empire of the Huns extends itself, embracing many conquered Germanic tribes ; seventy years later, under Attila, it threatens all Europe.

The Gothic colonists becoming discontented with the **375-8**
arrangements made for them, fierce disputes follow with
Roman officials, and war breaks out.   In the *battle of*
Adrianople, 378, Valens is defeated and killed, and the
dissolution of the Empire now really **begins.**

Its progress is for the moment retarded by Valens's
successor in the Empire of the East, **Theodosius** the
Great, who makes a compromise with the Goths, after
checking their advance, and recognizes them as ' allies of
the Empire ' officially settled within its borders in Moesia
(Bulgaria) and Thrace, 379.

Theodosius, a Catholic Christian, succeeding the Arian **379-95**
Valens, becomes the greatest lay head and protector of
the Church, as well as the most commanding and efficient
political force, since Constantine.

The **connexion of Church and State** *under Theodosius* is
illustrated by the following :

(*a*) The *Second* great *General Council* of the Christian **381**
Church, at Constantinople, 381, summoned by
Theodosius, completes the Nicene Creed, and *assigns*
to Rome the first, and to Constantinople the second,
place among Christian sees.

(*b*) *Theodosius, excommunicated by Ambrose,* Bishop **390**
of Milan, for barbarous cruelty in suppression
of a rebellion in Thessalonica, *does penance at*
Milan.

(*c*) *Theodosius prohibits Pagan worship* throughout the **392**
Empire.   Rapid decay of Paganism in the towns.
Its longer life in the country (*pagus*, hence
' Pagans ', &c.).

From 388, when he saves his colleague in the West,
Valentinian II, from dethronement, he is practically master
of the Roman World, and in 394 he *unites,* for a moment **394**
and for the *last time,* the *whole Empire under one head*

(except for the independent Gothic colony in Bulgaria
[Moesia] and Thrace).

395   But by the death of Theodosius, a year later, the **Roman
Empire** is **again, and for ever, divided** into Eastern and
Western sections.

1. Of these the **EASTERN,** which in later time (especially
after the outbreak of Islam in the seventh century) we
know as the **BYZANTINE EMPIRE,** and which is the sole
lineal successor of Old Rome throughout the Middle
Ages, lasts as one of the great states of the world till the
Turkish invasions of the eleventh century [see 1071, &c.],
and even till the Latin conquest of 1204 [see this year].

It is not finally destroyed till the capture of Constantinople by the Ottoman Turks in 1453

2. The **WESTERN EMPIRE,** on the other hand, becomes
completely the prey of the Northern Barbarians (Goths,
Vandals, Franks, Burgundians, Saxons, &c.) in the fifth
century, and the line of Western Roman Emperors is finally
extinguished in 476.

The so-called ' Restoration of the Empire ' in the West
by the Papal coronation of the Frankish king Charles the
Great (' Charlemagne ') in 800, and again by the coronation
of the German king Otto I in 962 (' the Holy Roman
Empire of the German Nation ' ; see 800, 962), are not,
of course, except in idea, revivals of the old Roman Empire
of the Caesars.   They are evidence—

(*a*) of the growth of the new nations of the West,

(*b*) of the influence of the old civilized tradition,

(*c*) of the influence of the Church.

The Empire, at the death of Theodosius, thus divided
between Arcadius (Arkadios)—who takes the East, and
has his capital at *Constantinople*, and Honorius—who
takes the West, and has his capital first at *Rome*, but after
402 at *Ravenna*—is attacked anew, and fatally, by the
Barbarians.

FIVE CHIEF MOVEMENTS OF THE NEW NATIONS   **395–410**

(a) Gothic ; (b) Vandalic, &c. ; (c) Frankish ; (d) Burgundian ; (e) Anglo-Saxon.

(a) The *Goths*, settled in the Balkan Peninsula, enraged at not getting their stipulated pay from Arcadius, rise under their king Alaric, ravage Macedonia, Greece, &c., establish themselves afresh in Illyria, and invade Italy without **401–8** decisive success, being checked by Honorius's guardian, the great general and statesman Stilicho, himself a Vandal.

Abolition of the gladiatorial shows at Rome and so, **402 (?)** within a few years, throughout the Empire. (Combats with beasts in arena continue longer.)

Death of St. John Chrysostom (b. 347 ; Patriarch of **407** Constantinople, 398), greatest of early Christian orators and one of the leading Greek Fathers, a very important and attractive figure in early Christianity.

Murder of Stilicho, by order of Honorius.   **408**

Death of Claudian (Claudius Claudianus, b. about 363), **408** often called the *last of the Latin classical poets*.

Fall of Rome. The Goths under Alaric again invade **409–10** Italy, besiege and retire from Rome, return, capture, and sack the city (410). ['Eleven hundred and sixty-three years after the reputed foundation of Rome, the Imperial city, which had subdued and civilized so considerable a part of mankind, was delivered to . . . the tribes of Germany and Scythia.'—Gibbon.]

(b) *Vandals*, Alans, Suabians (Suevi), &c., hard pressed by the Franks, leave their settlements in the Danube valley (406), *break into Gaul,* and thence make their way *into Spain, great part of which* (especially in South and West) *they conquer* [409, &c. ; now begins Mediaeval *Spain*] ;

(*c*) While the Salian Franks occupy much of Northern *Gaul* [now *France* really begins];

(*d*) The Burgundians part of Eastern Gaul, especially Alsace [here begins *Burgundy*]—both subsequently moving South, and

(*e*) The Saxons, Frisians, &c., raid part of Britain (' the Saxon Shore ', &c.).

The collapse of the old Roman Imperial system here shown by Honorius, in 410, releasing the inhabitants of Britain from their allegiance, as the emperor can no longer protect them. Already, in 401, the Roman troops have been withdrawn.

Note, that as the various Germanic tribes press into the Roman world and leave their original lands practically deserted, Slavonic races occupy the vacant territories, and thus **all the lands east of the Elbe** (and many regions to the west) **become Slavonic**. These lands are gradually conquered by the Germans, as far as the farthest limits of the old classical *Germania*, and far beyond, in centuries of struggle, especially from 928 to 1400 [see below, 928, 1134, 1226, &c.].

One chief interest of this period (375–410), as of those that precede and follow, lies in the **growth of Christianity and of the Church organization**.

Note especially :

(i) The development and importance of the Episcopal and Sacerdotal system.

(ii) The development of Sacramental doctrine, and of symbolic Ritual.

(iii) The development of Christian Monasticism ; at first mainly Oriental and centred in Egypt.

(iv) The progress of Christianity among the Teutonic and other invaders of the Empire [see above, 348, 375].

Immense impression produced by the fall of Rome.

Two things universally recognized :

(i) The collapse of the old political order in the West,
and

(ii) The triumph of Christianity. The two connected
as effect and cause by Pagan opinion. Christian
replies, especially by Augustine in the *De Civitate
Dei* (the ' City of Man ' has fallen ; but the ' City
of God '—the Church—remains).

Intellectual development of the Church at this time :

Augustine, Bishop of Hippo Regius in N. Africa [354–
430], greatest of the early Latin Doctors of the Church,
and a chief shaper of Roman theology ; Ambrose, Bishop
of Milan [340–97 ; see above], author of *Te Deum* (?) ;
Cyril of Jerusalem, 315–86 ; John Chrysostom, 347–407
[see 407].

Cyril of Alexandria, 376–444, an eloquent orator, a
virulent controversialist, an untiring organizer, and man
of affairs ; with Athanasius and Origen, the most famous
name in the Church of Egypt ; to his admirers ' the
Thirteenth Apostle '.

End of Latin classical poetry.

Claudian, 363–408; Rutilius Namatianus, fl. 400–15.

PERIOD III

FROM THE CAPTURE OF ROME BY THE GOTHS TO THE END OF THE ROMAN EMPIRE IN THE WEST (410–76)

GENERAL POINTS

1. The **Wandering of the Nations** is now **at its height.** The Northern invaders, Germanic and others, now begin their permanent settlements in Spain and Gaul [mainly Gothic], and in England [Anglo-Saxon] ; as well as their temporary dominion in Italy and Illyricum [mainly Gothic] and in North Africa [Vandal]. In this process they make an **end of the Western Empire.**

For a time the Huns threaten the destruction of all Europe, but this peril passes away after 452.

2. The storm of the **Barbarian invasions,** which first especially threatened the Eastern provinces, now passes by almost entirely to the **West** ; and the Roman **Empire in the East,** organized, governed, and led from Constantinople, each decade **becoming less Roman and more Greek and Oriental,** enjoys a long period of comparative peace, quiet, and prosperity.

3. In the shipwreck of so much of the Old Civilization, especially in the West, the **Church** becomes **constantly more important** as the saviour of every conservative and **cultured element.** The intellectual development of Christianity at this time is remarkable : in the earlier fifth century it reaches a higher point than at any time before the thirteenth. All this is interrupted and shattered by the success of the Barbarian invasions.

4. And one of the best auguries for the future of the West is that the **Barbarian Conquerors** begin so rapidly to pass over to **Christianity,** though at first mainly in the Arian form.

Six Chief Movements of the New Nations

(a) Gothic ;   (b) Vandalic ;   (c) Burgundian ; ·(d) Ala-
mannic ;   (e) Anglo-Saxon ;   (f) Hunnish.

(a) *Goths.*   After Alaric's death in South Italy, his **414, &c.**
brother-in-law and successor, Athaulf ('Adolf'), who
marries Placidia, the sister of Honorius, leads the Goths
out of Italy into Southern Gaul and Spain (a providential
deliverance to Honorius and his subjects), and founds the
Gothic dominion there.

Some of the Gothic leaders, it is said, aspired to blot out
Rome altogether, and erect on its ruins a Gothic capital and
empire.   They were gradually ' convinced that laws were
essential ' to the well-being of a state, and ' thought more
of restoring and retaining the Roman Empire than of
subverting it ' [Gibbon].

' Assuming the character of a Roman general ', Athaulf
' directed his march from the extremity of Campania to
the southern provinces of Gaul.'

Honorius grants *South Gaul to the Goths*, under imperial
suzerainty, 415 ;   thus arises

(a) the Visigothic kingdom of Toulouse, gradually
absorbed by the Franks in the sixth century, as
well as

(b) the *Visigothic kingdom of Spain,* with its capital at
Toledo, overthrown by the Muhammadans in the
eighth century [see 711].

[' The Goths first win for themselves a local habitation
and a place on the map when they leave Italy to establish
themselves in the further West.'—Freeman.]

The Visigothic pressure extends into the regions of
S. Spain, lately ruled by the Vandals.

Though the main Gothic force has now left Italy, the
imperial power in the West, in the last stages of its help-

lessness, rests upon Gothic and other Barbarian mercenaries, especially from 456, and these latter put an end to the Western Empire in 476.

429, &c.   (*b*) *Vandals.* From Southern Spain the Vandals and Alans, already settled here as conquerors [from 409, see above], cross over to Africa in 429, &c., led by the Vandal Gaiseric (Genseric), and conquer the greater part of 'Barbary' (Carthage falls 439). The Vandal kingdom of NW. Africa lasts over a century, 429–534, till destroyed by the Imperial Revival under Justinian.

Remarkable development of Vandal sea-power. Vandal fleets attack and pillage Rome (455), conquer some of the Western Mediterranean islands, and destroy the security of West Mediterranean commerce.

430   Death of St. Augustine of Hippo [see above, p. 13].

(*c*) *The Burgundians* moving southwards, out of Alsace or Elsass [see above, p. 12], settle in the lands of the later Duchy and County of Burgundy (valley of the Saône, &c.) ; while

443, &c.   (*d*) *The Alamanni* occupy the lands they [the Burgundians] have just vacated (modern Alsace, &c.), 443 ; and

449, &c.   (*e*) The Low German tribes of *Engles*, *Saxons*, and *Jutes* attack Britain, and begin the 'Anglo-Saxon Conquest' of the eastern part of the island (from 449).   Kent is probably the first region of the 'Saxon Shore' to be thoroughly subdued.

Lastly—

450-3   (*f*) *The Huns* (who served under Alaric, in great numbers) begin to move again (in their army are contingents of many conquered peoples).   Under their king Attila (Etzel) they

451   break into Gaul, besiege Orleans without success, and are defeated by a combined army of Roman troops, Goths, Franks, and Burgundians, under the Roman general Aetius, in the battle of Châlons-sur-Marne (' Catalaunian Fields ').

Repulsed from Gaul, the Huns next year throw them- **452**
selves upon Italy, destroy Aquileia, waste the North Italian
plain, but are induced to turn back by a Roman embassy
headed by Pope Leo I (' St. Leo the Great ').

Refugees from Aquileia and neighbouring coast lands,
flying before the Huns to the islands of the Venetian
lagoon, lay the *foundations of Venice.*

Death of Attila ; **break-up of the Hun Empire.**   **453**
The Hun invasions threatened the civilized world with
the same absolute barbarism, destruction of city life and
all culture, as the early Mongol conquests in the thirteenth
century [see below, p. 137, &c.]. Their defeat is therefore
of vital importance.

Meantime the 'Western Empire', now reduced to the
court of the nominal Roman Sovereigns in Italy, becomes
a puppet in the hands of the Barbarian Conquerors or
Mercenaries in Italy. Thus Attalus, made anti-emperor
by Alaric, on the eve of the fall of Rome, 409, convenes
the Senate, and announces his resolution of ' restoring the
majesty of the Republic' and uniting to the Empire the
provinces of Egypt and the East. Within a year he is
deposed by the Goths (410), and begs to be allowed to
follow the Gothic camp. At the wedding of Alaric's
successor, Athaulf, in 414, Attalus, ' so long the sport of
fortune and the Goths ', is chosen to lead the wedding
chorus, and ' the degraded emperor might aspire to the
praise of a skilful musician ' [Gibbon].

From 456 to 472 Italy is absolutely controlled by Recimir, **456–72**
the commander of the *Barbarian* mercenaries.

In 472–3 the Eastern Empire dictates the appointment **472–3**
of its western colleagues.

From 475 the army-leaders in Italy again control. And **476**
in 476 the *line of the* **Western Emperors** *becomes* **extinct** with
the deposition of Romulus Augustulus—himself a son of

the mercenary leader Orestes—by Odovakar (Odoacer), like Recimir, the chief of the 'Barbarian' generals in Italy.

By a vote of the Senate, the Western Empire is nominally reunited to the Eastern, the sovereign of Constantinople, the Emperor Zeno, being recognized as the sole chief of the Roman World.

Practically even Italy is now lost to the Empire.

Zeno recognizes Odovakar as master of Italy under the names of *Patrician of Rome* and *Praefectus Italiae*.

['The Senate disclaims the necessity, or even the wish, of continuing any longer the Imperial succession in Italy— the majesty of one monarch is enough to pervade and protect East and West alike. It consents that the seat of universal empire shall be transferred from Rome to Constantinople. The *Republic* (they repeat that name without a blush) might safely confide in the virtues of Odoacer, and they humbly beg that the Emperor would invest him with the title of *Patrician* and the administration of the *diocese of Italy.*'—Gibbon.]

GENERAL VIEW OF THE STATE OF EUROPE AT THE TIME OF THE EXTINCTION OF THE WESTERN EMPIRE (476)

The authority of Rome and the Roman political system have practically **ceased everywhere west of the Adriatic,** except in Northern Gaul.

The **Barbarian invaders,** mainly of German race, **rule** (with certain exceptions) in **every part of the Western provinces.**

I. As to GAUL :

(a) Part of Northern Gaul, from the Loire to the Somme, including all the Seine basin, still remains faithful to Rome, under the prefect Syagrius, successor of Aetius : it is soon to pass under Frankish rule.

As to the rest of Gaul :

(b) The *Franks* are masters of the North-East, from the Somme to the Rhine, with the Meuse and lower Moselle basins.

(c) The *Alamanni* control Alsace-Lorraine and the Upper Rhine basin from Mainz to the sources of the river.

(d) The *Burgundians* hold nearly all the South-East, including the basin of the Saone and of the Upper Rhone.

(e) The *West Goths* all the South-West, Middle-West, and extreme South, from the Loire to the Pyrenees, Mediterranean and ocean, including Narbonne and the coast of Provence.

(f) While the peninsula of *Brittany* (Armorica) is independent.

II. As to SPAIN :

Practically all the later kingdoms of Castile, Leon, and Aragon, together with South Portugal, are under the *West Goths,* except Gallicia.

C 2

Gallicia is in the hands of the *Suevi*, also masters of Northern Portugal.

The Asturias mountain-country in the far North is independent.

III. As to **ITALY** :

The whole country, in the Roman Imperial acceptation of the term (including much of modern Switzerland and the Tirol, and all Istria), together with most of Sicily, but not Sardinia or Corsica, forms the province of Odovakar, head of a motley crowd of Barbarian soldiers, mainly *Teutonic*, but including Slavonic and other contingents.

IV. As to **AFRICA** :

The *Vandals* rule from Tangier to modern Tripoli, and also in Sardinia, Corsica, the Balearics, and the extreme West of Sicily.

V. As to **BRITAIN** :

In the South-East, *Jutes*, *Engles* (English), and *Saxons* have begun to conquer and settle (from *c.* 449). The rest of Britain has already been without Roman protection or allegiance for nearly three-quarters of a century.

VI. As to **LANDS EAST OF THE ADRIATIC** :

The ' East Goths ' are settled (but only till 493) in what is now South-West *Hungary* and West and North *Serbia*. In 493 they move into Italy.

VII. As to the **EASTERN EMPIRE** :

In the **Eastern Empire**—the bulk of the *provinces beyond the Adriatic* (which, from the time of Diocletian, tend to be separately governed, separately considered, and reserved as the special dominion and residence of the emperor himself)—**no Barbarian settlement** of any importance has become permanent.

For the East Goths do not stay in SW. Hungary, but in 493 move on into Italy [see above].

At the beginning of the great migrations, and in the fifth century, it seems as if such a permanent settlement will be founded just south of the Danube, in what is the later *Bulgaria.*

But the Gothic tide has flowed away westward, and the frontiers of the Empire, below the present Belgrade, remain almost the same as they have been since Aurelian gave up Dacia.

A branch of the Gothic race ('Tetraxite') has settled in the southern parts of the Crimea, a region under the suzerainty of the Eastern Empire, and here they maintain a Germanic language, and something of Germanic life and custom, till the sixteenth century. In the thirteenth they have numerous and flourishing settlements.

In **ASIA** the (Eastern) Empire maintains practically the frontier of 363, retaining N. Mesopotamia and part of W. Armenia, with the region at the sources of the Tigris, but without recovering the trans-Tigris lands ceded after the death of Julian.

In **AFRICA** she now holds only Egypt and Cyrene.

State of the **CHURCH** at this time (*c.* 476). Immense **development** of its power and activity. Increase of its **adherents.** Perfection of its **organization.** Its **Councils** and **Missions.**

By the Council of Constantinople, 381, the rank of the great Bishoprics or *Patriarchates* has been settled : 1. Rome ; 2. Constantinople ; 3. Alexandria ; 4. Antioch.

By the Council of Ephesus, 431, the condemnation has been decreed of Nestorius and Nestorianism, an 'early and imperfect Protestantism' ; by the Council of Chalcedon (451), the last of the great general councils, acknowledged by all the Church, 'Monophysitism' has been put under ban.

[Nestorius and his followers emphasized the human nature in Christ ; objected to the term Theotokos, ' Mother of God ', applied to the Virgin Mary ; were accused by their opponents of undermining the doctrine of Christ's Divinity. The Monophysites represented an opposite extreme : they asserted one nature only in Christ, the divine.]

The Athanasian Creed is perhaps drawn up in this period in the Western Church.

Development of Papal Power in the time of Leo I, ' the Great ', and through his assertion of the **Petrine theory** [' Thou art Peter and upon this rock will I build my church ', applied to the claim of St. Peter, deriving from Christ a supreme position in the Church, which as Bishop of Rome he transmits to all his successors in the ' Apostolic See '].

Conversion of the Barbarians to Arian Christianity—

Of all the Goths (as we have seen, from Ulfilas, *c.* 348).

Of the Burgundians (from *c.* 460).

Of the Suevi or Suabians (in Spain, from 469).

Of the Vandals (from the beginning of the fifth century).

When the Franks are converted, in 496, to *Catholic Christianity*, they alone, among the new nations, profess it.   Hence the King of the Franks (and of France) is, later, ' Most Christian King ', ' eldest son of the Church '.

Meantime, Christianity, often of a heretical kind, especially **Nestorian,** has now spread very widely in Asia (and to a less degree in Africa), beyond the limits of the Roman Empire.

In Persia, India, and Central Asia—as in Abyssinia and Nubia—there are abundant traces of Christian churches and missionary enterprise before 476.

To this same time also belongs the conversion of the Irish by Patrick (from 432).

PERIOD IV

FROM THE END OF THE ROMAN EMPIRE IN THE WEST TO THE ACCESSION OF JUSTINIAN, 476–527

GENERAL POINTS

1. The creation of the great **Frankish state** by Clovis.
This is the inheritance of Charles Martel and Charles
the Great, the basis of the new 'Western Empire' of 800,
by far the largest and most powerful of the new nations
as now formed.

2. The **Conversion of the Franks** to Catholic Christianity
secures the ultimate triumph of Catholicism in Western
Europe over both Heathenism and Heretical (especially
Arian) Christianity. It also prepares the way for that close
alliance of the Franks with the Church of Rome, which is
one main cause of the new Western Empire of 800.

3. Something like a real Italian state promises to be
developed through the Ostrogothic Conquest. But this
promise proves a mirage.

4. The **Anglo-Saxons win all Eastern Britain,** and definitely
make good their position in the country, which through
them becomes England (*Engla-land*).

The [Eastern] Empire at this time, and for half a century previous, under Zeno (474–91), Anastasius (491–518), and Justin (474–527), is externally uneventful, but internally prosperous.

Formation of a fresh army of native levies.

Adequate defence of the frontiers.

Reforms in taxation and administration. Far-reaching economies. Accumulation of vast state reserve-funds.

Useful public works (e. g. the great wall protecting the district of Constantinople from Euxine to Propontis).

c. 477 First definite establishment of the Saxons in England (the South Saxons in Sussex).

Capture of the great Brito-Roman fortress of Anderida, or Pevensey, guarding all this part of the south coast.

481–6 **Clovis** (Chlodwig, Chlodovech), 481–511, of the Merwing or Merovingian House, King of the Salian Franks, conquers the last relics of Roman Gaul, the prefecture of Syagrius in the north. Battle of Soissons, 486. By this the Frankish power becomes supreme over all Northern Gaul.

489–93, &c. Immediately after this, **Theodoric** and his people, the East Goths or Ostrogoths, settled to the north-east of the Adriatic [see above], are commissioned by the Emperor Zeno to overthrow and replace Odovakar (489). They accept and execute the commission (493), thereby establishing a Gothic Arian dominion in Italy (493–553), and relieving the Eastern Empire of most of the Gothic pressure on the north-west of its territories (the Serbian-Montenegrin-Bosnian regions of to-day). The rule of Theodoric, ' the Barbarian Champion of Civilization ', 493–526, shows the deep and rapid effect of Roman civilization upon the northern invaders. He carefully fosters every trace of the ancient culture, and endeavours to make one people of Goths and Romans. His work is hindered by both racial and religious differences, the Goths remaining Arians.

In politics, Theodoric (who stops the Vandal raids upon Italy and makes peace with the Vandals) gradually becomes the great protector of the Goths against the ever-rising power of the Franks.

[Some have even seen the promise of a genuine Italian Kingdom in Theodoric's work : ' Only in the nineteenth century has Italy regained that national unity, which might have been hers, before it was attained by any other country in Western Europe, if the ambition of emperors and popes, and the false sentiment of Roman patriots, had spared the goodly tree . . . planted in Italian soil by Theodoric the Ostrogoth.'—Hodgkin.]

The conquest of Hampshire is now begun by the West **c. 495** Saxons under Cerdic and Cynric [*Chronicle* tradition].

The Franks, meanwhile, united under Clovis, and masters **496–511** of the whole north plain of ' France ', from Loire to Rhine, next proceed to

1. The conquest of the *Alamanni* in *Alsace-Lorraine,* 496.
2. The conquest of the *Burgundians* in the Dijon region, 500.
3. The *defeat of the West Goths and their expulsion from W. Gaul,* down to the Garonne, 507, and nearly to the Pyrenees, 508. The Gothic dominion in the extreme south of Gaul (Septimania and the coastal strip, from the Rhone to the Pyrenees, and from the Rhone to the Alps) is saved by the defence of Arles, and the intervention of Theodoric, who unites Provence with his own dominion, and acts as guardian for the young West Gothic king in the rest of the latter's dominions.

After the victory over the Alamanni, in 496, **Clovis and 496 his people accept Catholic Christianity.** Clovis and his court baptized by Bishop Remigius at Rheims (' Burn what thou hast adored : adore what thou hast burned'). *With this begins the Catholicizing of the Teutonic World ; all the future history of Western Christendom is vitally affected by this.*

505 Christianity in China (earliest historical evidence : see below, p. 30).

510 The Roman Consulship is bestowed on Clovis by the Emperor Anastasius.

511 On the death of Clovis, the supreme power is divided (not by territorial partition) among his four sons, who jointly rule the Frankish state and people from the court-towns of Metz, Orleans, Paris, and Soissons.

c. 520 The West Saxon advance in Britain is checked, and the invaders are kept for the next twenty years to Hampshire.

523 Final conquest of Burgundy by the Franks.

At the end of his life Theodoric is embittered by his failure to conciliate his Catholic Roman subjects in Italy and his discovery of conspiracies against his rule. He therefore in 525 executes the Senators Symmachus and Boethius, whose *De Consolatione Philosophiae* is often considered as the *latest work of ancient philosophy and even of classical (prose) Latin*, at a time when classical style was pretty nearly extinct. Theodoric's minister, Cassiodorus (c. 470–562), statesman, historian, orator, educationalist, encyclopaedist, writes his *History of the Goths*, the earliest formal history of a Germanic race, preserved only in the Abridgement of Jordanes (' Jornandes ').

Progress of Christianity.

Extinction of Classical Paganism : its last traces above ground in the West belong to the age of Theodoric, who enacts death for the practice of Pagan rites. In the East, Theodosius II, long before this, in a law of 423, affected to question whether there were any Pagans left. Philosophical Paganism lingers on to the time of Justinian [see p. 31].

PERIOD V

THE AGE OF JUSTINIAN, 527-65

1. The **Revival of the Empire,** both in political power and civilized activity (literature, law, architecture, &c.), is the outstanding feature of this time. But Justinian's wars, court, buildings, &c., prove terribly expensive : his maladministration exhausts the state.

2. A temporary check to the rising Papal power is administered by the restored imperial authority in Italy.

3. **Progress of Western Monasticism.**

4. Progress of the **Anglo-Saxon Conquest of Britain.**

The Eastern Empire, for some time relieved from Hunnish and other northern dangers, maintaining its frontier against Persia, consolidated and strengthened by rest, economy, reform, and consequent prosperity, the result of one hundred and twenty years of good government from the death of Arcadius (408), now passes under the control of a ruler of vast ambitions. Justinian himself is perhaps of Slavonic origin, like (?) his uncle and predecessor, Justin, and like (?) Belisarius, the ' Africanus of New Rome'. (It is **now we first come clearly upon the Slavonic stock** in Mediaeval history. One of the earliest mentions of the name is in Procopius.)

The new emperor aims at restoring to the Empire something of its Roman and universal character by a reconquest of the West. Aided by *ministers and generals of extraordinary ability* (the Graeco-Levantine John of Cappadocia ; the Roman Tribonian ; the Slav (?) Belisarius ; the Persian (?) Narses), as well as by the obvious decline of the Vandal power since the death of Genseric (477), and by the weakening of the Gothic kingdoms (through the death of Theodoric, 526, the renewed separation of East and West Goths, and the feeble and turbulent minority of Theodoric's grandson and successor), *Justinian achieves a great measure of success*—

(i) Externally, (ii) internally.

(i) *External.*

1. First, the *reconquest of Africa*. The imperial armies under Belisarius attack and overthrow the Vandal dominion in NW. Africa and the Mediterranean Islands, 533–5. Thus the *Empire again extends to the Ocean* (Tangier), again takes in all the best part of Roman Africa, and again controls important lands of Latin speech (the *earliest important Latin theology*—Cyprian, Tertullian—is to be found in the *African* lands conquered by the Vandals).

2. Next, the *reconquest of Italy* is undertaken.

(*a*) First conquest, by Belisarius, 537–40 : defeat and

captivity of Vitiges, King of the Goths.   Gothic
revival under Totila, 541–4.

(b) Second, imperfect, conquest of Italy by Belisarius,
544–8 ; his final recall, 548.

(c) Third and final imperial attack upon Italy under
Narses ; his complete success ; the East Gothic
State destroyed, 552–3 ; invasion of Franks and
Alamanni repulsed, 554 ; all Italy restored to the
Empire.

Six years before this, in 548, Provence has been ceded
to the Franks.

The reconquered Italy is governed from Ravenna, like
the Ostrogothic kingdom, but now by a Byzantine viceroy,
the Exarch.   The line of the Ravenna Exarchs, beginning
with Narses (553–67), lasts two hundred years (till c. 752),
when the Byzantines have finally lost all their possessions
in North and Central Italy.   (From this latter time, the
middle of the eighth century, the Papal State, in a measure,
begins to take the place of the Byzantine dominion.)

3. Thirdly, the *reconquest of part of* Southern *Spain* is
effected, at the cost of the West Goths, while the struggle
with the East Goths is in its most critical stage, c. 550.

The Roman dominion is thus again extended round the
greater part of the Mediterranean, including both Old and
New Rome and the whole of the original Latin country—
Italy ; and though the Empire is no longer the only power
in the Mediterranean World, it is obviously the predominant one.

Also the recovery of so much Latin territory does something to check the Graecizing or Orientalizing of the Empire,
and to restore to it something of its old universal character.
But, by the middle of the eighth century, little of this
is left.

4. In the East, a long and fierce but indecisive struggle

is waged with Persia, now ruled by the greatest of the
Sasanidae, Chosroes 'the Just' (Khusru *Anushirvan*,
531–79). Struggle for the control of Lazica or Colchis
(the modern Batum and Poti region, at the extreme
east of Black Sea). Close attachment of the Crimean
Goths (threatened by the Turks soon after 553) to the
Empire.

Immense and well-executed system of frontier defences
carried out by Justinian, especially against Persia, but
also on a great scale in the Balkan peninsula, in Africa,
and in the Crimea.

His attempts to form alliances against Persia—
   (i) With the Abyssinian Christians (embassy of Non-
       nosus to Abyssinia, 533, &c.).
  (ii) Perhaps even with Indian powers, and
 (iii) With the Turks.

Intercourse between the Empire and India during this
period. ' Romans ' in *Ceylon*.

Intercourse with races of Central Asia—e.g. the Avars,
migrating into Europe and flying before the *Turks, who
now* also *touch the horizon of the Western world* for the first
time.

Indirect intercourse with *China*.

(ii) *Internal.*

Internal and economic state of the Empire. Agriculture,
trade, and industry. Vicious imperial finance ; extrava-
gance balanced by parsimony ; crushing taxation to meet
enormous expenses, often caused by wastefulness and
negligence. *Exhaustion of the Empire* at the close of
Justinian's reign. Famine and pestilence, especially in
541, &c. Importation of the *first mulberry silk-worms from
China* into the Roman Orient by ' Persian ' (? Nestorian)
monks, long resident in the Far East, *c.* 552 [earliest
evidence of Christianity in China 505]. Rapid progress
of the new silk manufacture in the Mediterranean World.

(Hitherto the West had only known the silk-worms of pine, oak, and ash trees, generally neglected, except in Cos, where men spun the ' Coan silks ' of antiquity.)

Architecture. Justinian's buildings—*this is the great age of East-Roman or Byzantine Architecture.* The patriarchal church of *Hagia Sophia* [*The Sacred* or *Divine Wisdom*] at Constantinople, originally founded by Constantine, now rebuilt by Justinian, 552-8, the most magnificent of Christian temples before the Crusading Age. (' Solomon, I have surpassed thee.')

Many other churches (twenty-five in Constantinople alone), palaces, and buildings of this time. Immense system of fortresses.

The factions of the Circus. The ' Nika ' sedition of 532.

The Empress Theodora : her influence.

The historian Procopius, his works on the *Vandal, Gothic,* and *Persian Wars* and on the *Buildings of Justinian*; his scurrilous *Anecdotes*, a satire on Justinian and Theodora. Anthemios of Tralles, Isidore the Milesian, and other architects of St. Sophia, &c.

The lawyer Tribonian.

Justinian's suppression of the Schools of Athens (the chief ' University ' of Classical Antiquity and the last refuge of Philosophical Paganism) ; also of the Roman Consulate, 529-41. [The Benedictine Monks begin at this very time, see below.]

Law. Justinian's Legislation—the reformation and codification of the entire body of Roman Law, begun in 527, and mainly effected by Tribonian, with nine colleagues—one of the chief landmarks in the history of civilization.

['Caesar I was, and am Justinian,
  Who by the force of primal love I feel,
  Took from the laws the useless and redundant.'
                    Dante, *Paradiso*, vi.]

530-65   *Development of the Frankish Empire.*

Conquest of *Thuringia* by the Franks, with the aid of the Saxons, 530-2.

561   Fresh division of the Frankish kingdom into four parts :

1. *Austrasia*, with Rheims for capital.
2. *Neustria*, capital Soissons.
3. *Burgundy*, capital Orleans.
4. The later *Île de France*, capital Paris.

The last is in 567 divided up among the three former, and this triple division lasts till the seventh century.

563   *Colom* (Colomba, Columba), crossing from Ireland, lands *in Iona* and founds there a mission-station, which becomes the head-centre of the Irish Missions in Britain, and (in later times) the earliest metropolitan see of the Scottish Church. The next century (to about 664) is the age of the *highest activity of the Irish Church*, and of its most brilliant *successes in the mission-field.* [' For a time it seemed as if Keltic and not Latin Christianity was to mould the Churches of the West.']

Striking *intellectual, especially artistic, developments accompany the Irish mission-activity,* and continue in full activity till the eleventh century. Not till the twelfth does Ireland come into the Roman obedience.

540-65   *Progress of the Anglo-Saxon Conquests in Britain.*

Resumption of the West Saxon advance in the South from about 540 (?) [*Chronicle* tradition ; see 520].

Conquest of Wiltshire and Berkshire.

East Saxons spread over much of Essex and Middlesex, *taking London.*

English conquests in the extreme North (Lothians of Scotland) from the Firth of Forth and the East Coast.

Ida, ' the flame-bearer ', the *first great Northumbrian chief,* 547.

Conquest of parts of East Anglia, Yorkshire, Lincolnshire, the Midlands, &c., by various English tribes.

[Anglo-Saxons still all heathen—till 597.]

In the general *Church History* of this time, we notice the

(*a*) *Progress of the conversion of the northern invaders* **520–70**
    from Arianism to Catholic Christianity [soon, by
    c. 600, only Lombards remain Arian].

(*b*) *Temporary subjection of the Roman see to effective
    Imperial Control*, once more, after the recovery of
    Rome by Belisarius. [Deposition and exile of Pope
    Sylverius, 537.]

(*c*) *Spread of Christian Missions*, mainly Nestorian, *in
    Further or non-Roman Asia*; evidence of Nes-
    torianism now flourishing in *Malabar*, and even in
    Ceylon [limited perhaps to the Persian commercial
    colonies], e. g. in

    Cosmas ('Indicopleustes'), the Indian and African **535–47**
    traveller. His system of ' Christian cosmography ',
    an attack on the doctrine of a round or spherical
    world and an attempt to substitute a ' scriptural '
    conception (a supreme example of anti-scientific
    spirit in early Christianity).

(*d*) *Progress of the New Monasticism in the West.* **495–**
    Benedict of ' Nursia ', i.e. Norcia in Spoleto (480– **528, &c.**
    543), founder of the *Benedictines*, the greatest and
    most extensive of all monastic orders, from which
    immediately sprang the Cluniac, Carthusian, Cis-
    tercian, and other revivals—these orders being
    nominally reformed Benedictines. Benedict's her-
    mit-life near Subiaco *c.* 495, &c. Beginnings of
    the parent monasteries of Subiaco and Monte
    Cassino, midway between Rome and Naples, 510,
    528. The Benedictine rule drawn up about 529 (cf.
    the suppression of the Schools of Athens this year).

PERIOD VI

FROM THE DEATH OF JUSTINIAN TO THE RISE OF ISLAM, 565–632

GENERAL POINTS

1. **Relapse of the Empire** under Justinian's successors.

2. **Invasion of Italy** and permanent conquest of great part of the country **by the Lombards.**

3. Desperate **struggles between the Empire and Persia,** ending in the defeat of the latter, and the exhaustion of both combatants.

4. More definite appearance of the Turks in relation to Europe—as allies of the Empire against Persia.

5. **Renewed strength of the Papacy.**

6. **Completion of the Anglo-Saxon conquest of Britain. Conversion of the English.**

7. The **rise of Islam** (the faith preached by the Prophet Muhammad) in Arabia.

The full significance of this is seen in the next period, when Islam breaks out of Arabia on its mission of world-conquest, and wins such advantage from the weakened state of the Empire and of Persia.

Though not wholly lost till the eleventh century, when **567-70** the Normans extinguish the last remains of the Byzantine Empire in South Italy, Justinian's gains in the West are practically destroyed within one hundred and fifty years (by A.D. 700) ; in Italy the 'East Roman' dominion is undermined within a single decade of Justinian's death [565-75]. **In civilization** there is a **terrible set-back between Justinian and Leo the Isaurian** (565-717).

The Teutonic *Lombards* ('Langobards' or 'Longbeards', **568-72** who in alliance with the non-Aryan *Avars* have just destroyed the Teutonic *Gepid* kingdom in modern Hungary, 566-7) *break into Italy and conquer the greater part of the interior*, especially the great northern plain, called 'Lombardy' henceforth after them, and the regions of Spoleto and Benevento.

The Empire, however, retains much of the coast, especially the four districts near (1) Ravenna, (2) Venice, (3) Naples, (4) Rome, (5) the extreme south, (6) the Italian islands.

The very *incompleteness of the Lombard conquest* is important for the history of Italy. Imperial and Lombard possessions are left so intertwined that *no* sort of *National Unity* is possible. Thus by a Lombard conquest there is no real restoration of the Teutonic kingdom of Italy ; on the other hand, the *infusion of new blood* completed by the Lombards does much to make a New Italy (in the Commercial Republics, &c.).

The *Lombard* migration is one of the *last incidents* of the *first* and principal *chapter of the Wandering of the Nations*.

A *second chapter* follows later with *Scandinavian* and *Hungarian* migrations.

The Frankish Empire remains divided into *Austrasia*, **567-613** *Neustria*, and *Burgundy*, forecasting the later and more permanent division of France, Germany, and a middle kingdom [see 843]. *Austrasia* is mainly Teutonic : *Neustria*

D 2

and *Burgundy* are mainly Romance : towards the North Sea, the river Scheldt divides Teuton and ' Roman ' elements.

568, &c.   A *Turkish alliance*, the chief asset of Byzantine policy under Justin II, is formed from about 568 ; it is especially directed against Persia.

Embassies exchanged between Constantinople and Central Asia ; the great *Khagan* or *Khan* (' Dizabul '), visited by the Byzantine envoys, seems to have had his court in the Altai.

572–4   After the murder of Alboin, the first Lombard king in Italy (said to have forced his wife Rosamund to drink from her father's skull, and to have perished by her revenge), the Lombards soon break up into a confederacy under chieftains or ' dukes ', without a supreme head. This is probably an important check to the progress of the invaders.

575   Fresh embassies exchanged between Constantinople and the Turks.

576–9   (Mainly) victorious war of the Empire, allied with the Turks, against Persia.

Byzantine troops on the Caspian.

577   Battle of Deorham. Victory of the West Saxons over the *Britons*, who are *divided by the Saxon conquest* of this region (Bath, Gloucester, and Lower Severn valley) into two main sections. The *English* conquerors now *reach the western sea* at the Bristol Channel.

585   Beginnings of the *alliance between the Franks and the Church of Rome against the Lombards*, and earliest Frank invasion of Italy in this cause.

585   Visigothic conquest of Spain completed : absorption of the Swabians in the NW.

586–9   Complete *conversion of the Visigoths* from Arianism *to*

*Catholic Christianity. Of the Northern races within the old
borders of Empire, only the Lombards now remain Arian.*

Northumbria, founded by the union of Deira (Yorkshire) **588**
and Bernicia (Durham, Northumberland, and East Lothian
to the Forth), soon becomes the leading English state.

Greatness of Kent. Supremacy of its king, Æthelberht, **590**
over all SE. England. Value of this in furthering the
conversion of the English (from 597).

The Emperor Maurice (Mauritios) restores the Persian **590–1**
king, Chosroes the Younger (Khusru Parviz), to his throne.
Persian cessions to the Empire.

Pontificate of Gregory I (' the Great ').   **590–604**

Death of St. Columba, founder of the Irish religious **597**
house at Iona and leader of the Irish missions in Britain.
His name gains an influence in the Irish Church second
only to that of Patrick [see 563].

A *Roman mission,* under Augustine, dispatched by Pope **597**
Gregory *to England,* lands in Kent. It relies first on
the help of the Frankish princess, Bertha, Æthelberht's
queen.

Early successes of the Roman mission in Kent, Essex, **597–627**
and Northumbria (627).

Murder of the Emperor Maurice by the usurper Phokas. **602**
The Persians attack the Empire, 603 ; as time goes on
they gain the alliance of the Avars, settled in (our) Hungary
[see above, 568].

Death of Pope Gregory the Great [see 590].   **604**

Importance of his pontificate. (*a*) The imperial power
becomes more shadowy in Rome. The Church tends to
take its place. (*b*) Thus the Roman Church approximates
to a temporal power ; its head to a temporal sovereign.
(*c*) A vast missionary movement among the (still heathen)
Teutonic peoples, beginning with England, is organized

from Rome : this somewhat compensates Christendom for her losses to Islam, and does much to form modern Europe. (*d*) Though studiously moderate in his assertion of Papal claims ('Away with words that puff up vanity and wound charity '), Gregory stands out as the real working head of the whole Christian Church of his day. (*e*) He is important in the history of Christian theology, liturgy, ritual, music ('Gregorian tones', &c.). Reputation of his *Dialogues*, his *Magna Moralia* or commentary on Job, and his *De Cura Pastorali* (or *De Regula Pastorali*) throughout the Middle Ages. Translation of the latter into Anglo-Saxon by Ælfred the Great. In theology, Gregory ranked with Augustine, Ambrose, and Jerome, as one of the four Latin 'Doctors of the Church'. (*f*) In his time Arianism everywhere gives way before Catholicism, even among the Lombards. Gregory's extant Letters—more than *800* in number—show his work as an administrator, and illustrate his ubiquitous and incessant activity ; 'his capacity for business ; his wide, varied, and minute supervision ; his dexterity and tenacity in the conduct of affairs'. He has his word in almost all the important ecclesiastical matters of W. Europe, and in many of the secular. 'From the highest concerns of Church and State he passes to direct the management of a farm, the reclaiming of a runaway nun, or the relief of a distressed petitioner in a distant province.' To all his other gifts he added the saving grace of humour.

608-19   Momentary Persian conquests from the Empire—Damascus, Jerusalem, Antioch, and most of Syria, Palestine, Asia Minor, and Egypt. Great destruction of historic monuments, and especially of the Christian buildings of Constantine and Helena in Jerusalem (614). Constantinople threatened from the Asiatic side (Persian camp at Chalcedon), while the Avars threaten it in Europe. Peril of the Empire.

Muhammad begins to preach his faith ('Islam') at Mecca **609**
[see 622].

The Northumbrian *English*, under Æthelfrith, rout the **613**
Britons at Chester, conquer this region, and thus *split the*
British lands into three (as Deorham had broken them into
two), penetrating to the western sea at the mouth of the
Dee, &c.

Supremacy of Northumbria, under Eadwine, over nearly **617–32**
all the English (except Kent) and some of the Britons—
a *first* real *approach to a 'kingdom of England'*.

Death of Columban, the chief of the Irish missionaries **615**
on the continent of Europe in this century. Columban is
active in France, the Rhine-land, Switzerland, and N.
Italy.

Eadwine of Northumbria [perhaps] founds *Eadwine's* **c. 617**
Burh, Edinburgh, by the fortification of the Castle Rock.

The *Mayors of the Palace* begin to dominate the Frankish **c. 620,**
courts. The *Karling or Carolingian family* concentrates in **&c.**
itself the power of this Mayoralty.

The Emperor Heraclius takes the field against the Persians **622**
in Asia Minor with brilliant success (but till 626 they do
not retire from Chalcedon).

Muhammad ['Mohammed', i.e. 'The Praised'; in Turk- **622**
ish 'Mahomet'], rejected and in danger of his life at Mecca
[Makkah], **flies to Medina** [Al Madinah], where he is well
received, and begins to gain an important following.
From this centre he gradually wins all Arabia. This *flight*
is **the Hijra** or *Hegira*, from which Muhammadans begin
their chronology.

The Arabic Peninsula had never hitherto been effectively
united for any purpose ; it was inhabited by tribes which
mostly owned a certain racial affinity and a common
religious belief—a vague nature-worship, especially of

the heavenly bodies, centred at the Temple in Mecca—
the ' Kaaba '—where was the famous meteorite known as
the ' Black Stone '. Arabia now undergoes the decisive
change of its local history, and, as the result of this, effects
one of the chief revolutions in world-history. Muhammad,
born about 570 at Mecca, belonged to the Kuraysh,
a family at the head of the Arabian aristocracy, which
dominated the sacred city and guarded the Kaaba.   He
himself, however, before his marriage with his cousin
Khadijah, was poor, and of small account. For some time
he is said to have been a camel-driver in Khadijah's service.
In 609 [see this year] he *begins to preach as the apostle and
prophet, not* (as he claimed) *of a new faith, but of the ancient
belief* of all the prophets (' Hear, O Israel, the Lord thy
God is one Lord '). This faith, now revived and reformed
by himself, last and greatest of the prophets, the con-
summator of the work of Abraham, Moses, and Christ, is
Al Islam, the *Making of Peace* (by submission to the will of
God ; cf. s'lam, ' salaam '). Those who hold it are *Muslims*
(' Moslems '), i.e. those *who have Made Peace* (by such submission).

Issue, by many successive chapters, of the **Kuran**
[Koran] or Sacred Book of Islam.

Islam has one fundamental principle—' I testify that
there is but *one God* '—and an essential sub-principle—
' and that *Muhammad* is the *Apostle and Prophet of God* '.
It enjoins four practical duties : (*a*) *Prayer,* five times
a day ; (*b*) *Fasting,* during the thirty days of Ramadan,
from sunrise to sunset ; (*c*) *Almsgiving,* one-tenth of the
income of every believer ; (*d*) *Pilgrimage,* to Mecca [and
Medina] once in the life of every believer.

Friday is the Muhammadan day of public worship. The
Kaaba of Mecca is the Kiblah, or point to which all turn
in prayer. Wine and pork are forbidden. Slavery and
polygamy **(four wives and unrestricted concubinage)**

allowed.   Emphasis on future life : salvation of all Muslims.
No proper priesthood, no sacrificial system, and (in a sense)
no miraculous claims, in Islam.   Priesthood of all believers.

Islam or Muhammadanism, though historically the great
rival of Christendom and its civilization, itself renders
service, in various countries and times, **to civilization**
(especially in its earlier, Arabic, period, and among Asiatic
and African races).

The *early Muslim culture*, brilliant from the ninth to the
eleventh century A.D., almost extinct after the fourteenth,
devotes itself particularly to poetry, mathematics, and
natural science (astronomy, medicine, &c.).   From *Muslim
schools* (e.g. in Spain and Baghdad), and by Muslim scholars
in Christian lands, the *knowledge of Christendom* is much
advanced.

Final joint Persian-Avar attack on Constantinople repulsed.   **626**
Continued victories of Heraclius in Armenia, Mesopotamia,
Media, &c.   Persians retire from the Bosphorus.

Conversion of the Northumbrian court (Eadwine) by the   **627**
Roman mission [see 597].

Peace between the Empire and Persia.   Frontiers restored   **628**
as before the war (603).   Exhaustion of both combatants.

Muhammad begins to attack the outer world by a raid   **629**
upon the Empire in Palestine.

Muhammad compels Mecca to surrender, and prepares   **630**
to attack the Empire in force.

All Arabia submits to Muhammad and embraces Islam.   **630–2**

Death of Muhammad (June 8) in the middle of his pre-   **632**
parations for attacks upon Persia and the Empire.

PERIOD VII

FROM THE RISE OF ISLAM AND THE BEGINNING OF THE ARABIAN INVASIONS TO THE HIGHEST POINT OF MUHAMMADAN WORLD-CONQUEST, 632–732

GENERAL POINTS

1. The **outbreak of Islam as a world-power** creates the new empire of the Arabs under the *Caliphs* [Khalifahs] or *Successors* of Muhammad. This great revolution completes the change from ancient civilization to the mediaeval. From this time we see Christendom and European civilization for centuries struggling against an Asiatic reaction and a new aggressive religion. Early Islam thus tears away from Christendom many of its richest lands, containing some chief centres of Mediterranean life and culture ; greatly injures and hampers Christian trade and intercourse ; confines the horizon, and depresses the spirit of Christendom.

2. The **Byzantine Empire,** when almost succumbing to the Muhammadan attacks, is **saved** by the new ' Isaurian ' dynasty (Leo III), and **thereby saves Christendom in the East.**

3. The **Frankish power,** directed by the new Karling line of Viceroys or *Mayors of the Palace*, under Charles Martel, repels the Muhammadan advance north of the Pyrenees, and **thereby saves Christendom in the West.**

4. **Victory of Christianity in England.** Defeat of the Pagan reaction. English rejection of Irish Church allegiance for **Roman.**

5. The English, Irish, and other missions on the Continent begin to win Central (especially the purely Germanic) Europe for Christianity : the English missionaries help to make this Christianity Roman.

6. Progress of Mediaeval Thought. A partial Renaissance of Learning.

7. The Karling House of *Mayors of the Palace* practically dethrone the House of Clovis.

8. A close alliance is developed between the Church of Rome and the new Frankish dynasty.

632   After the death of Muhammad, Abu Bakr is elected as his *Caliph* [*Khalifah* or 'Successor'] to command the Faithful. The Islamic movement of world-conquest is only delayed for a short time by the loss of the founder. Revolts against Islam in Arabia quickly suppressed. Authorized and completed 'publication' of the *Kuran*, which had been issued by Muhammad, section by section, during the last twenty or more years.

633   Momentary victory of the Pagan reaction in England, headed by Penda of *Mercia* (the Western Midlands). Defeat and death of Eadwine of Northumbria in the battle of Heathfield, 633. Mercian supremacy over all Middle England.

633-7   **Arab conquests** in Palestine and Persia. Umar or 'Omar', the second Caliph, 634-44, leading figure among early Muhammadan statesmen. Persian defeat at Kadesia, 636 ; the Sasanid royal standard taken. Roman defeats in Palestine. Capture of Damascus (635); of Jerusalem (637); and of Ktesiphon, the Persian capital (637). Foundation of the earliest mosque at Jerusalem (the first *Aksa*), at the south end of the Jewish temple-area : the present *Aksa* and ' Mosque of Omar ' were built about A.D. 690, &c.

635-42   Partial restoration of Northumbrian and Christian power in England under Oswald.

636   Death of Isidore of Seville, the chief Christian encyclopaedist of the ' Dark Ages '. His *Etymologies* or *Origins*, as a compendium of universal knowledge, is a standard text-book even to the thirteenth century.

638-9   Conquest of North Syria by the Arabs ; fall of Antioch.

639-41   Invasion and conquest of Egypt by the Arabs, with some [alleged] help from Coptic Christians, forming the bulk of the native population, who had been constantly treated as heretics by the emperors. Capture of Alexandria, so long the second city of the Mediterranean World

(Rome till Constantine, Constantinople after Constantine, being first).

The Muslim conquest of Egypt cuts off the European supply of the ancient paper or papyrus (from about this time). Its place is partly taken by the costlier ' vellum ' (prepared skins of animals) ; see 1450.

Tradition of the destruction of the Alexandrian Library **641** by the Muhammadan Conquerors. Omar's alleged decision : ' If the books of the Greeks agree with the Book of God (the *Kuran*) they are useless and need not be preserved : if they disagree, they are pernicious and should be destroyed.' This doubtless exaggeration, perhaps altogether a fabrication (but cf. the burning by Muslims of Zoroastrian books in Persia). The Alexandrian Library, the greatest and richest collection of the ancient Mediterranean World, had already much declined since the age of the Antonines. But it does disappear from history under Muhammadan rule.

Battle of Nahavand. Final *destruction of the old Persian kingdom* of the Sasanidae (founded A.D. 226), which later *becomes the central part of the Caliphs' empire*, containing the capital, Baghdad, after the accession of the House of Abbas in 750.

Surrender of Caesarea. Complete conquest of Syria by **642** the Saracens. (Thus, nearly one thousand years after the first European conquest of the Levant, by Alexander the Great, European ascendancy is destroyed in Syria and Egypt by the Asiatic reaction.)

Renewed triumphs of the Pagan reaction in England. **642, &c.** Oswald of Northumbria defeated and killed, in the battle of Maserfield, 642. Mercian supremacy extended over much of S. England.

Muhammadan conquest of ' Barbary ' (N. Africa beyond **647** Egypt) begins.

Decisive *victory of Christianity in England*.   **655**

Penda defeated and killed by the Northumbrians under Oswiu at the battle of the river Winwaed (near Leeds). Northumbrian supremacy extended over all Northern and Central England (to the Thames).

Triumph of Irish Christianity in the north.

659   Successful revolt of Mercia, under Wulfhere.

Final destruction of Northumbrian leadership in England. Movement towards national unity checked. England seems falling into a triple division—North, Midlands, South.

661   The House of Umayyah [the Umayyad or ' Ommiad ' dynasty] succeeds to the Caliphate with Muawiyah, who changes the supreme Muhammadan power from elective to hereditary.

664   The rivalry between Roman and Irish missions for the allegiance of the *English decided in favour of Rome* by the Synod of Whitby. All England thus brought into relation with the main body of Western civilization.

665, &c.   Renewed progress of Muhammadan conquest in N. Africa (Barbary) after a prolonged pause.

669   Theodore of Tarsus sent from Rome, as Archbishop of Canterbury, to *organize the Church in England*. His work (669–90), admirably carried out, helps towards real national unity and sentiment. The ' *Church of England* ' *leads to the ' Kingdom of England* '.

c. 674-6   First unsuccessful Muhammadan siege of Constantinople. *Earliest recorded use of Greek Fire* (the mediaeval predecessor of gunpowder), invented shortly before this (by Kallinikos of Heliopolis in Syria ?). Among the ingredients of ' Greek fire ' were naphtha, sulphur, pitch. ' From this mixture, which produced a thick smoke and a loud explosion, proceeded a fierce and obstinate flame,' which burnt with equal fury upwards and downwards. Water only increased its energy. Sand and vinegar were among the few things that could extinguish it. Till about 1100 the Eastern Empire kept the secret : it was then discovered or stolen by the Muhammadans, who used it on the Crusaders. The composition of 'Greek ', ' maritime ', ' wild ', ' wet ', or ' liquid ' fire has been lost for several centuries.

Final ruin of Carthage. In its place, foundation of **c. 675** Kairwan (' Cairoan ') in Tunis. The great mosque here, one of the first important works of early Muhammadan architecture and art, served in some measure as a model for Cordova [see p. 72]. *Muhammadan conquest,* led by Akba, triumphant in Barbary, *reaches the Atlantic Ocean.* [' Great God, if my course were not stopped by this sea, I would still go on to the unknown kingdoms of the West, preaching the unity of Thy holy name, and putting to the sword the rebellious nations who worship any other gods.']

Cædmon of Whitby, the *earliest recorded English poet,* **c. 680** writes *On the Beginning of Created Things.*

Renewed advances of the West Saxons from this year. **682** Expansion of Southern England at the expense of the Britons of Somerset, Devon, &c.

English (Northumbrian) aggression upon Picts, N. of **685** Firth of Forth, decisively checked in the battle of Nectansmere. *Beginnings of a great Pictish or* **Scottish** *state.*

Battle of Testri. The ' Karling ' House (that of Charles **687** Martel, Pippin [Pepin], and Charles the Great) definitely acquires the Mayoralty of the Palace or headship of the royal household—the practical sovereignty—in the whole Frankish kingdom.

Willibrord, the pioneer of the Anglo-Saxon missions on **690** the Continent, which do so much to win Central Europe for the Church, begins his work in Frisia (N. Netherlands).

' Doges ', Dukes, or Sovereign Mayors, of **Venice** first **c. 690–** recorded. About the same time the line of Doges begins **700** at **Amalfi.** These are the pioneers in the commercial life of the Christian Mediterranean, especially of Italy.

691 or 692   Council of the Church ' in Trullo ' marks the beginnings of severance between Greek (Eastern) and Latin (Western) Churches (e.g. the Roman Church rejects decrees of this council permitting the clergy to marry and asserting the equality of the Bishops of Rome and Constantinople).

695–715 ?   Muhammadan conquest of Cilicia and of Cyprus (part ceded by Treaty of 686).

c. 700   Complete expulsion of Byzantine rule from North Africa, and subjugation of N. African Christianity, which henceforth rapidly decays.

Native risings against the Muhammadan Conquerors in Barbary suppressed by 709.

c. 710–720   Chinese paper introduced via Central Asia to the Muhammadan world.

711–13   **Muhammadan** *invasion and* **conquest of Spain** under Tarik and Musa. Seizure of Gibraltar [Jibal Tarik, Hill of Tarik]. Battle of Xeres.

Overthrow of the Visigothic Monarchy. Capture of the chief Spanish towns ; all the Peninsula occupied up to the northern mountains (Pyrenees, Asturias). Extraordinary rapidity, ease, and duration of Muslim conquest here.

Till the thirteenth century the best parts of Spain remain Muhammadan : till about 1000 nearly all Spain. Christian reconquest is not absolutely complete till 1492. Remarkable developments of Muhammadan culture in this country.

714   **Charles Martel,** ' the Hammer ', becomes Mayor of the Palace, i.e. practical Viceroy, in the Frankish State (retains this till his death in 741).

708–16   The Muhammadans overrun great part of Asia Minor, reach the Bosphorus, and threaten Constantinople.

716   Winifrith of Crediton, otherwise ' St. Boniface ', the English Apostle of Germany, begins his work on the Continent (Utrecht, Thuringia).

Second and **decisive Arab siege of Constantinople** (lasting **717-18** twelve months). The city is saved by the general **Leo the Isaurian,** who, as the Emperor Leo III, becomes the founder of the ' Isaurian ' and ' Iconoclast ' dynasty (717-800). The Caliphate really puts out its strength (army of 180,000 men, fleet of 2,600 war vessels and transports) in this great effort, and its defeat is a crucial event for Europe and Christendom in the East.

(Take this event in connexion with the battle of Tours, 732. Had either of the main Islamic attacks succeeded it is not difficult to imagine the complete conquest of Europe and Christendom. Had both triumphed, ' a victorious march might have carried the Saracens to Poland and Scotland. . . . Perhaps the Koran would now be taught in Oxford.'—Gibbon.)

Muhammadan invasion of S. France. Momentary con- **718, &c.** quest north to Bordeaux, east almost to Marseilles. Finally, after the Duke of Aquitaine has been defeated, all Aquitaine is overrun : flying Saracen bands spread to Tours, Lyons, even Besançon.

But between Poitiers and Tours the main Saracen army **732** is met by Charles Martel and the Franks, and in a seven days' running struggle utterly defeated—the so-called **Battle of Tours, which saves Christendom in the West,** as the **defence of Constantinople** had **saved it on the East.**

During these years the Byzantines under Leo the **718-32** Isaurian are gradually recovering Asia Minor, a possession vital to the Empire, and are regaining control of the sea.

About this time early *Irish art* reaches its highest development, e.g. in the manuscripts and their illustrations. The *Book of Kells* (seventh to eighth century) and the *Book of Durrow*, which professes to have been written by St. Columba himself (before 597), are perhaps the most celebrated examples of this early Irish art.

PERIOD VIII

FROM THE BATTLE OF TOURS TO THE REVIVAL OF THE WESTERN EMPIRE, 732–800

GENERAL POINTS

1. The Byzantine Revival is maintained—down to the death of Constantine V. After this, the Eastern Empire weakens again somewhat.

2. The Isaurian emperors become involved in a bitter struggle with most of Catholic Christendom, and especially the Church of Rome, on the *Iconoclast question*.

3. The usurpation of Irene completes the **movement of revolt in the West.** The Church and people of Old Rome repudiate allegiance to a female usurper [see 6].

4. The **Karling House,** dominating the Frankish kingdom, displaces the Merwing, or Merovingian dynasty (the House of Clovis), and **seizes the Frankish throne.**

5. The new Frankish dynasty binds still more closely the alliance with the Church of Rome, and *destroys the Lombard power in Italy.*

6. The Pope, Church, and people of Rome claim to declare the Empire vacant, and to appoint the Frankish king in place of the deposed Byzantine empress. Coronation of Charles. **Commencement of a new Western Empire.**

7. Progress of the Roman Mission movement on the Continent.

8. **Revolution in the Caliphate.** Dethronement of the Umayyads. Accession of the Abbasids. Revolt of Spain. Disruption of the Muhammadan Empire. Foundation of Baghdad.

9. Development of the Mediaeval Philosophy of the Church.

Progress of the Byzantine *Imperial Revival under Leo the* **732, &c.** *Isaurian* [see 717].   Military, financial, commercial, and legal reforms.   Reconquest of Asia Minor.

Death of Baeda (the Venerable Bede), the first important **735** man of letters and science among the English.   His work for civilization [history, theology, science, scholarship] continued in various Northumbrian Schools, especially at York and Jarrow (in Durham).   First among ' English scholars, historians . . . theologians, it is in the monk of Jarrow that English learning strikes its roots ' [see 740]. Bede does much to revive the credit of the 'Pagan' doctrine of the roundness of the world, ' like the yelk in an egg '.

 [' See farther onward flame the burning breath
  Of Isidore, of Beda. . . .'
         Dante, *Paradiso*, x.]

Charles Martel, on the death of the Frankish king, rules **737** alone, without nominal sovereign, yet without taking the royal title himself.

Great Byzantine victory over the Saracens.   **739**
Reconquest of Cyprus about this time (?).

Prosperity of the School of York under Archbishop **c. 740–** Ecgberht.   Alcuin was a pupil (afterwards the head) of this **756** School [see 801, 804].

Deaths of Charles Martel and Leo the Isaurian.   **741**
Pippin [Pepin] ' the Short' becomes Mayor of the Palace at the Frankish court.

The Anglo-Saxon Boniface, ' Apostle of Germany ' [see **741** p. 53], missionary bishop among heathen Germans from 730, is commissioned by Pope Zacharias to reform the Frankish Church, and does so with energy and some success.

Boniface made Archbishop of Mainz and ' Primate of **746** Germany ' ; under him are the bishops and dioceses of Worms, Speyer, Tongres, Cologne, Utrecht.

750   Revolution in, and **disruption of the Caliphate** [cf. the dynastic revolution in the Frankish kingdom, 751]. The *Umayyad* (' Ommiad ') dynasty overthrown by the *Abbasid* [descendants of Abbas, uncle of Muhammad]. Spain won to the Umayyad cause by Abdurrahman I (755–63), the practical founder of the **Western Caliphate** [in name only an *Amirat*, till 929, when Abdurrahman III assumes the style of *Caliph*]. The *loss of Spain* is followed, after a time, by the *loss of Africa*.

751   *Dethronement of the Merovingian or Merwing line of Frankish rulers* (House of Clovis) to make way for the House of Charles Martel, Pippin, and Charles the Great (the **Karling** or Carolingian **dynasty**). ' Karling ' kings do not wholly cease to reign in West Frankish (French) lands till 987 : in East Frankish (German) lands they end 911. Karling emperors reign 800–88. *Share of the Papacy in this revolution* : Pope Zacharias, consulted as to ' whether the real or nominal rulers ' should have the sovereign title, answers ' the former '. This Papal action, though often described with exaggeration, is important, and foreshadows the developments of Papal temporal power in the next centuries. Boniface of Mainz said to have crowned Pippin.

c. 752   The Byzantine Viceroys in Italy (' Exarchs ' of Ravenna) come to an end through Lombard conquest.

755   The Franks, under their new dynasty, are appealed to by the Papacy for help against the Lombards (who have just completed their conquest of the Byzantine Exarchate, and dominate Italy). They invade the peninsula, defeat the Lombards, and take from the latter various territories, which they hand over to the Roman Church. This *Donation of Pippin* is usually considered as the **foundation** (it is at any rate an essential development) **of the temporal power of the Papacy.** But the gifts of this donation appear to have been held by the Church of Rome *under the Frankish Crown.*

Muhammadan rule completely destroyed in France : the **c. 755** last Saracen invaders driven beyond the Pyrenees.

Partial revival of Christian Spain. New kingdom of Asturias (later Leon and Castile) formed under Alfonso I, 750–5. A considerable part of Northern Spain (down to the Douro) temporarily recovered from Islam.

Martyrdom of Boniface near Dokkum in Frisia. Impor- **755** tance of the career of the 'German Apostle'; his foundation of mission-sees as far east as Passau and Salzburg.

Death of John of Damascus, one of the chief forerunners **760** of **Scholasticism.**

[The work of the *Schoolmen*, among other things, attempted :

1. To systematize Christian Theology as a science.
2. To comprise and treat all knowledge under the head of Theology.
3. To adapt Ancient Philosophy (e.g. Aristotle) to the uses of Christian Theology.

Scholasticism, which reached its height in the thirteenth century, occupied many of the ablest thinkers of the Middle Ages, and in some of its work, e.g. the *Summa Theologiae* of Thomas Aquinas, has left a lasting memorial in the history of human ideas.]

The capital of the Abbasid Caliphate moved from **762, &c.** Damascus to **Baghdad,** which remains **the capital of Eastern Islam** till the Mongol conquest of 1258.

Death of Pippin. Accession of **Charles** ('**the Great**', **768** 'Charlemagne') to the Frankish throne. He has already been joint ruler with his father and brother from 754.

Charles becomes sole ruler of the Franks after the death **771** of his brother Carloman.

Charles begins the conquest of the heathen Saxons on **772** the north-east, between lower Elbe and lower middle Rhine.

c. 772   Pope Hadrian I begins the use of the forged *Donation of Constantine* by the Roman popes—calling on Charles the Great ' to imitate the liberality, and revive the name of . . . the first of Christian Emperors '.

773–4   Charles, again summoned by the Papacy to aid against the Lombards (' that perfidious and most unsavoury nation '), *finally destroys the Lombard power in Italy*, and makes a *fresh Donation to the Church of Rome*, especially of the Ravenna region.

> [' And when the tooth of Lombardy had bitten
> The holy Church . . .
> Did Charlemagne victorious succour her.'
>
> Dante, *Paradiso*, vi.]

775   With the death of the able and ruthless soldier-iconoclast, Constantine V (' Kopronymos '), the Isaurian revival of the Eastern Empire, which had driven the Saracens out of Asia Minor and Cyprus, and the Bulgarians out of Thrace, begins to lose strength.   The Iconoclast movement also declines with the death of this hated champion of early Puritanism (his enemies ' exhausted the bitterness of religious gall in their portrait of this spotted panther, this antichrist, this flying dragon of the serpent's seed . . . ').

778   Charles begins to attack Spanish Islam on the south-west (the ' Saxon war ' is still raging on the north-east) [see 772].

779   **First** recorded **Scandinavian** (' Viking ') **attack on Western Europe :** descent on the Bordeaux region.

780–5   First Frankish conquest of the Saxons completed by Charles.   Forcible ' conversions '.

782   Alcuin, from the School of York, joins the court of Charles the Great.   In the ' Carolingian Revival' of Letters, Alcuin, Paul the Deacon (the historian of the Lombards), and Einhard, the biographer of Charles himself, are noteworthy figures.

Foundation of the Great Mosque at Cordova by Abdur- **785** rahman I [see 990].

Harun ar Rashid [' the Just '], the most famous Abbasid **786** Caliph, begins to reign at Baghdad.   His friendship with Charles, to whom he sends presents of silk stuffs, perfumes, drugs, musical instruments, and rare animals, especially an elephant.` Charles's gifts are of Frisian cloth, furs, and amber. Harun's reign (786–809) appears in Muslim tradition and romance (e.g. the *Arabian Nights*) as a *golden age of Muhammadan* power, *splendour*, and culture.

First Scandinavian descents on English coasts.   **787-93**

The Second Council of Nicaea ends the Iconoclastic **787** controversy in favour of the ikons, and the ' ikon-wor- shippers '.   But no real reconciliation follows with the Church of Rome.

Charles's wars with Scandinavians (Danes, Viking raiders, **789** &c.), and with the Slavs beyond the Elbe.

Charles's successful wars with the (Turco-Tartar) Avars **791-6** in modern Hungary, especially between Danube and Theiss.

A fresh Frankish attack upon Muslim Spain.   **795**

First recorded discovery of Iceland, by Irish monks, who **795** notice the perpetual daylight of midsummer (' no darkness to hide a man from doing what he liked ').

First recorded landing of Scandinavian invaders in **795** Ireland.

Buildings of Charles the Great at his court-town of **c. 796,** Aachen (' Aix-la-Chapelle ').   From his palace chapel (on **&c.** the pattern of St. Vitale at Ravenna), where he was buried, the cathedral was developed.

The Byzantine Empress-Mother Eirene deposes and **797** blinds her son, Constantine VI, thus ending the Isaurian dynasty.   The Church of Rome repudiates allegiance to a female Caesar of such infamy, and prepares, in effect, to revive the separate Western Empire, extinct since 476, in the person of the Frankish king and people. [As to the theory of Old Rome on this point, see below, 800.]

799   Scandinavian raid in Aquitaine—the first serious Viking attack on the Frank Empire [see 779].

800   **Charles crowned emperor in St. Peter's at Rome by Leo III** on Christmas Day.   [' The church rang to the shout, *Karolo Augusto a Deo coronato magno . . . imperatori vita et victoria.*   In that . . . was pronounced the union, so long in preparation, so mighty in . . . consequences, of the Roman and the Teuton, of the memories and civilization of the south with the fresh energy of the north', and here a new age of history begins.—Bryce.]   This revolt of the Church and people of Rome from the historic Empire is represented by them and their supporters as a mere *Translátio Imperii* (from the Eastern Rome back to the Western, from the ' Greeks ' to the Franks, legally effected by the vote of the Church and people of Old Rome).

PERIOD IX

FROM THE REVIVAL OF THE WESTERN EMPIRE TO THE PARTITION OF VERDUN, 800–43

GENERAL POINTS

1. Decline and ruin of the new Western Empire after the death of Charles.

2. **Beginnings of ' Modern Europe ' with the partition of Verdun,** by which the Western Empire is divided into three parts. With these begin the history of (*a*) ' Modern France ', (*b*) ' Modern Germany ', (*c*) Burgundy and the ' Middle States ', now represented by Holland, Belgium, Switzerland.

3. At the same time we have the **earliest official monuments of French and German speech** (Oaths of Strassburg, &c.).

4. The civilizing movement fostered by Charles the Great in great measure collapses. **One of the darkest of the Dark Ages** is the ninth century from the death of Charles.

5. **First** real approach to a **' kingdom of England ',** under West Saxon leadership.

6. The Scandinavian raids increase in extent and violence, and **Scandinavian colonization begins** on a large scale.

7. Steady progress of **Christian missions.**

8. Beginnings of **higher Muhammadan culture** in the (eastern) Caliphate, especially at the court of Baghdad.

801   Fresh Frankish attack on Muhammadan Spain. Conquest of Barcelona.

801   Alcuin retires from the court of Charles the Great, becomes Abbot of St. Martin-at-Tours, and there organizes a School somewhat on the model of York.

802   Ecgberht (founder of the West Saxon headship of all England) becomes King of the West Saxons.

804   *Final conquest of the Saxons* of N. Germany by the Frankish Empire, which now includes all the Germans of the homeland.

804   Death of Alcuin, the principal scholar and writer of the age of Charles the Great, and one of the leading churchmen and diplomatists of the Frankish State and Western Empire [see 801, 740].

811   Nikephoros I, Eastern Emperor, defeated and killed by the Bulgarians, who from this time till the accession of Nikephoros Phokas (in 963), and the beginning of the great ' Byzantine military revival ', are a serious danger. Their power is not seriously weakened till 969–71.

c.810–20   Muhammadan conquest of Corsica and Sardinia, from the Eastern Empire, about this time, or a few years earlier.

823   Muhammadan conquest of Crete from the Eastern Empire (by a raid from Spain). Crete remains a Saracen pirate-lair, with terrible results to Christian, and especially Byzantine, trade, till its re-conquest by the Eastern Empire in 960 [which see].

825–6   Ecgberht's victories over Mercians (Middle English) : the men of Kent, Sussex, Essex, East Anglia, accept West Saxon overlordship.

826   Anskar (Ansgar), ' Apostle of the North ', begins a Catholic mission among the Danes.

Muhammadan conquest of Sicily begins : most of the **827** island, with Syracuse, won by 878 ; but in the north-east corner the Byzantine resistance is not over till 965.

Mercians and Northumbrians submit to West Saxon **827** overlordship. **Ecgberht first real Over-King of all the Anglo-Saxons** (a real unified ' kingdom of England ' still distant).

Civil war breaks out in the Western Empire, ruinous to **829** the State, through the disputes between the children of Lewis ' the Pious ' (grandsons of Charles the Great) over their inheritance.

A Catholic mission begins in Sweden under Anskar [see **829** above, 826].

Anskar, archbishop of new (missionary) metropolitan **831** see of Hamburg (and Bremen).

Scandinavian attack upon SW. England, in alliance **836** with Britons of Cornwall, &c., repulsed by Ecgberht.

Death of Ecgberht. Scandinavian attacks upon England **839** soon increase in violence.

Death of Claudius (bishop) of Turin, ' iconoclast and **839** demi-Protestant '. His writings often curiously anticipate points raised by Wycliffe, Hus, and the sixteenth-century reformers.

The Scandinavians, who have been harrying and settling **c. 840,** in Ireland since at least 795, now begin a conquest of the **&c.** whole country. This marks a departure in policy. Ireland is the first foreign country where they attempt a complete subjugation.

Increasing violence of Scandinavian attacks on the **c. 840–3** Western Empire, especially within ' French ' lands. Rouen taken, 841 ; Nantes, 842 ; Northmen winter at mouth of Loire [their first wintering on Frankish soil ?] 843.

During all this time (800–43) the Scandinavians, beginning with ravages, have gradually mastered and settled in
the Hebrides, Orkneys, Shetlands, and Faroes.

840   Death of Lewis the Pious :

> ' Rex Ludovicus pietatis tantus amicus,
>   Qui *Pius* a populo dicitur et titulo.'

[' He left the empire he had done so much to dismember
to be fought for by his sons and grandson.'—Oman.]

841   Battle of Fontenay. Defeat of Lothar, representing the
unity of the Empire under one imperial overlord, by Ludwig
(Lewis) the German and Charles the Bald, who represent
the separation of the German and French nations in the
Western or Frankish Empire, and who may be considered
the first kings of ' Germany ' and ' France '.

842   The Oaths of Strassburg (to bind closer the alliance of
Ludwig and Charles). This is the **first important official
monument of French and German speech.**

843   **Partition of the Western Empire by the Treaty of Verdun.**
Hereby is created a **French,** a **German,** and a **Middle**
kingdom.

1. The French kingdom, under Charles the Bald, answers
in all respects to the mediaeval kingdom of France, as
it existed without much change till about 1310–14—
bounded by the Ocean, the Channel, the Mediterranean,
the Pyrenees, and Spanish March, the Cevennes, Rhone,
Saone, Meuse, and Scheldt (almost nothing east of these
rivers). Brittany may perhaps be considered as independent. The Spanish March is soon lost.

2. The German kingdom, under Ludwig the German,
roughly lies between the Rhine and the Elbe, but includes
certain lands (in the neighbourhood of Mainz, Worms, and
Speyer) on the west side of the Rhine, and does not include
Friesland or any of the east Rhine-bank below Koblenz.
The eastern border advances slightly beyond the Elbe **in**

Holstein, but falls westward of the Elbe to the south of (later) Magdeburg. In the Danube valley it again advances east to just below (modern) Vienna, and thence drops down to the Adriatic immediately east of Istria. This border is not greatly changed on the east till after 920.

3. The Middle kingdom, under Lothar, includes all Frankish Italy ; most of Burgundy ; Provence, part of Languedoc ; Friesland ; most of the land between the Rhone and the Alps on one side, and between the Rhine and the Scheldt, Meuse, and Saone, on the other. The two capitals of Charles the Great, Aachen (Aix-la-Chapelle) and Rome, are included in the *Middle kingdom*. Lothar's anxiety to get good wine-producing land, in the partition, is one alleged cause of the strange shape of this Middle State.

From (1) mediaeval and modern France has resulted ; from (2) Germany ; from (3) the Burgundies, and the states of N. Italy, Switzerland, Belgium, Holland.

Union of Picts and ' Scots ' (originally colonists from **843** Ireland) under Kenneth II.

Development of a ' Scottish ' realm [see 685].

PERIOD X

FROM THE VERDUN PARTITION TO THE FINAL DISRUPTION OF THE FRANKISH EMPIRE, 843–88

GENERAL POINTS

1. **Final disruption of the new Western Empire** in its **Frankish** form.

2. **Zenith of Scandinavian activity**—raiding, conquering, colonizing.
Settlements in England, Ireland, Iceland, Netherlands, &c.

2 *a*. **Beginnings of the Russian nation** through Swedish migration, and the resulting Scandinavian conquest and leadership of Slavs.

2 *b*. **English revival** under Ælfred the Great. Partition of England between the West Saxon State and the Scandinavian conquerors.

3. Decisive **breach between the eastern and western** ('Greek' and 'Latin') parts of the **Church**, mainly arising from

4. **Growth of Papal power** and Papal claims, especially under Nicolas I.

5. **Progress of Christian missions.**

6. **Growth of Feudalism.**

Scandinavian attacks upon Muhammadan Spain (espe- **844**
cially Lisbon and Seville) and upon Marocco.

All the three states of the Verdun Partition—'France', **845**
'Germany', and 'Lotharingia'—are attacked by the
Scandinavians ('From the fury of the Northmen, good
Lord, deliver us ').

Pope Leo IV, dreading a capture of Rome by Saracen **849**
raiders (whose activity increases terribly in Italy after the
Frankish civil troubles begin in 829), fortifies 'the Leonine
city', thus enclosing St. Peter's and the chief shrines of
Christian Rome, on the Vatican hill. At the end of the
fourteenth century, after the return from 'Babylonish
captivity' at Avignon, the Vatican becomes the Papal
residence [see p. 186].

Line of able and aggressive popes, 847–82, culminating
in Nicolas I, 858–67.

Miserable state of Western Christendom, at this time **c. 850**
attacked by Scandinavians on north, by Slavs and others
(Hungarians a few years later) on east, by Muhammadans
on south—the Western Empire hopelessly divided—feudal
disintegration everywhere.

Composition of the *False Decretals* [see 860].   **c. 850–**

Death of the Emperor Lothair. His son, Lewis II, reigns **855 (?)**
as nominal emperor to 875.   **855**

Scandinavians first winter in England (in Sheppey).   **855**
Pressure of their attacks upon all Western Europe.

Nicolas I, Pope, one of those pontiffs 'who stand **858–67**
forth in history as having most signally contributed to the
advancement of their see'. Assertions of the spiritual
power over the civil by Nicolas I, especially in the case of
Lothair II, King of Lotharingia, whom he compels to take
back his divorced wife (865). Nicolas is pictured by
a contemporary as surpassing all his predecessors since

Gregory the Great ; as commanding kings and tyrants, and ruling them as if lord of the world ; as gentle to the worthy, terrible to the refractory, as another ' Elias in spirit and in power '.

Progress of a more aggressive Papalism [see 867].

858-61   Scandinavian attack upon Muhammadan Spain and raids in the Mediterranean.

c. 860   The *False Decretals* [see 850-5] are brought to Rome and adopted by the Papacy. ' Fifty-nine Decretals, which purported to be those of the Popes of the second and third centuries, and thirty-nine more . . . interpolated among the real documents extending from Siricius to Gregory II (384-731). There was also in this precious collection the . . . *Donation of Constantine*. . . . To any one with . . . knowledge of early Church history, or textual criticism, the *False Decretals* would have betrayed their character at once. . . . It is impossible not to suppose that Nicolas I knew what he was doing in accepting ' them, but they ' were too tempting to be neglected ', and so were ' at once incorporated in the authentic . . . Acts of Councils, edited by Isidore of Seville ' [see p. 44]. ' Who forged the pseudo-Isidorian Decretals we ' may ' never know. They were first heard of at Mainz ', and probably composed ' at Mainz or Rheims '. ' A mouse-trap for Metropolitans ' they are called by Hincmar of Rheims, the greatest ' Metropolitan ' of his time [see 882], ' because they threw all ' ultimate ' power into the hands of the Roman Pontiff ' [Oman].

c. 860   Scandinavians (Northmen) reach Iceland.

860-930   Harald ' Fairhair ' (' Haarfager '), king in Norway, crushes the petty kings, and unites all the states in one kingdom. Many leave home to escape his rule, and join the roving colonists (Vikings) already spread over so much of the seas and coasts of Europe. An immense increase

of Scandinavian expansion-activity thus results from the
unity and consolidation of Norway.

Scandinavian migration from the Upsala region of **c. 862**
Sweden to Old Novgorod in NW. Russia.
Beginnings of the Russian nation.

Cyril and Methodius, apostles of the Slavs, begin their **863**
mission work in Central Europe (Moravia, upper valleys
of Drave and Save, &c.).

Conversion of the Bulgarians in the Balkan Peninsula.   **861–6**
Struggles between Rome and Constantinople for their
allegiance. The Patriarch **Photius** (of Constantinople) ;
his services to learning, literature, history, &c. His
Myriobiblion. His work in the conversion of Bulgaria.
His controversies with Rome—denunciations of enforced
celibacy of clergy, &c.

Rupture (practically **final**) **between** the Churches of Rome   **863–7**
and Constantinople—between **Greek and Latin Christianity.**
[' Nicolas styled Photius an intruder and usurper . . . and
declared him deposed. . . . That one patriarch should
. . . remove . . . another without . . . a General Council, and
merely . . . as the successor of Peter, appeared monstrous
to the Byzantine clergy. . . . After seven years of wrangling
the division between East and West was finally formulated
by the Synod of Constantinople (866), where the Emperor, **866**
the patriarch, and 1,000 bishops and abbots drew up the
Eight Articles. . . . The Third . . . denounced the enforced
celibacy of the priesthood as a snare of Satan . . . the
Seventh . . . condemned the Roman doctrine of the pro-
cession of the Holy Ghost, " a heresy deserving a thousand
anathemas ".' Photius was afterwards deposed (September 867) ; restored 877 ; afresh excommunicated by Rome,
whom he defied, 879 ; finally deposed after death of Basil I
(886), ' but his fall did not heal the breach, for the Byzantine
emperors and clergy . . . adhered to the statements of . . .
1765
                    F

the Synod of Constantinople. To this day they are held by the Eastern Church.'—Oman.]

The Papal claims were, of course, the fundamental reason of the schism. Nicolas I developed these afresh, beyond the standard of Leo I or Gregory I, and strained matters till a rupture resulted.

867   Basil I seizes the throne of Constantinople and founds the longest and most glorious of Byzantine dynasties (the 'Basilian' or 'Macedonian', largely of Armenian blood).

Death of Pope Nicolas I. Importance of his pontificate. ['The increase of the Papal power under him was immense. He had gained such control over princes as was before unknown. He had taken the unexampled steps of deposing foreign metropolitans, and of annulling the decisions of a Frankish National Council by . . . a Roman synod. He had neglected all the old canonical formalities . . . in the way of his exercising immediate jurisdiction throughout the Western Church. And in all this he had been supported by the public . . . indignation against Lothair and his subservient clergy.'—Robertson.]

867–78   Great **Scandinavian** attack on England.

Conquest of all England N. of Thames. Wessex almost crushed, but saved by a national uprising under its new king **Ælfred** (871–901) in 878.

874   *Permanent Scandinavian settlement in Iceland* begins. Remarkable *civilization* (literature, especially) developed here.

Icelandic Sagas—in their present form of eleventh–fourteenth centuries (*Burnt Njal, Eyrbyggia, Red Eric*, &c.).

Iceland becomes a base for further Scandinavian discovery and settlement—Greenland, Vinland, &c.

875   Death of the (nominal) Emperor Lewis II. Charles the Bald, 'first King of France' [see 843], receives the imperial crown.

Alleged Scandinavian discovery of Greenland (?) [see **c. 877**
910].

Death of Charles the Bald [see 843, 875].   **877**

Death of John Scotus Erigena, the *first mediaeval philo-* **c. 877**
sopher of real originality, and one of the leading thinkers of
the Middle Ages. Probably a native of Ireland. He often
works in scholastic method, but his outlook and purpose
are really philosophical, quite independent of theological
views. He shows a remarkable knowledge of Greek. For
many years he lives at the court of Charles the Bald [from
c. 843 ?], and is head of the palace-school.

Peace of Wedmore. England divided between the Scan- **878**
dinavians in N. and NE. and Wessex in S. and W.
Scandinavian England, ' the Danelaw ', includes all the
North and the Eastern Midlands. Ælfred keeps (1) all
south of Thames, (2) the Western Midlands (all west of
Watling Street).

Charles the Fat (son of Lewis the German and great- **881**
grandson of Charles the Great) receives the imperial crown.

Kiev becomes the capital of the Slav-Scandinavian **882**
Russians, and the seat of their Grand Princes till 1169 [see
862, 1169, 1240].

Novgorod, though deserted by the ruling clan of the *Rus*,
maintains a distinctive and rival position, and becomes the
chief Russian trading town.

Death of Hincmar (b. 806 ; Archbishop of Rheims, **882**
845–82), ' a man of strong, lofty, and resolute character,
of a mind at once subtle and eminently practical, of learning which . . . raised him above almost all his contem-
poraries, and of great political talent. . . . He steadily
upheld the Church against Crown and nobles. . . . But
especially he was the champion of the national Church
and . . . his sovereign against . . . the Papacy.' In his
character are suggestions both of Bossuet and Talleyrand,

'Il y a de l'évêque de Meaux et un peu de l'évêque d'Autun.'

c. 852–
86

Growth of Feudalism in France. In all 'the "Great Fiefs" the first commencement of hereditary rule dates from the fatal days between . . . Fontenay and the deposition of Charles the Fat. . . . In Toulouse it dates from 852, in Flanders the date is 862, in Poitou 867, in Anjou 870, in Gascony 872, in Burgundy 877, in Auvergne 886' [Oman].

'**Feudalism** may be understood as a social and political organization based upon **land-ownership,** and upon the personal relations created by that land-ownership. Its **theory** required (i) that he who held land of another was his immediate subordinate and owed him the service of a vassal to a lord ; (ii) that every free man under the King should have a lord ; (iii) that any man, not holding land at all, was in a state of dependence or serfage ; (iv) that all land was ultimately held of the King, who was the apex of the social and political pyramid '.

884–7   Momentary reunion of Frankish States—France, Germany, Lotharingia, Italy, &c. (all except Southern Burgundy)—under the Emperor Charles the Fat.

[This temporary and expiring reaction against the Nationalist tendencies shown at Verdun, 843, &c., is of no importance.]

884–6   Renewal of struggle between Wessex and the ' Danes '. Defeat of the Northmen. Advances of Wessex.

New Wessex-' Danelaw ' boundaries : up Thames and Lea to sources of latter near Hertford ; thence to Bedford on the Ouse; thence to line of Watling Street, crossing Ouse near Stony Stratford.

885   Great siege of Paris by the Northmen. Defence of the city by Odo (Eudes), Count of Paris, son of Robert the Strong and ancestor of the House of Capet [see 987]. Here the *importance of Paris in history begins.*

Charles's dishonourable treaty with the Northmen, and **887-8** obvious incapacity, lead to his deposition.

Final disruption of the Frankish States, and re-commencement of the separate life of France, Germany, Italy (*France and Germany never again united*). In Germany Arnulf of Carinthia (887–99) elected king by the *East Franks*.

In France one party among the *West Franks* elect Odo as king (888–98) ; the legitimist or Karling party elect Charles the Simple (893–923).

About this time the *Magyars* or Hungarians, a race of **c. 887-8,** Finnish (non-Aryan) stock, which had entered Europe by **&c.** way of the Lower Volga and the Steppes (north of the Euxine), cross the Carpathians and *overrun Hungary*. Thence they attack Germany and Italy. (' From the arrows of the Hungarians, good Lord, deliver us.')

PERIOD XI

FROM THE FINAL DISRUPTION OF THE FRANKISH EMPIRE TO THE COMMENCEMENT OF THE GREAT GERMAN KINGDOM OF THE MIDDLE AGES, 888–919

GENERAL POINTS

1. **End of the Carolingian Empire.** The separate states resume their **separate activities** and development—Germany, France, Italy, Burgundy.

2. Depressed state of nearly all Christendom, especially in the West. This is **one of the darkest of the Dark Ages** (888–919).

3. A partial exception to the general depression is found in the Eastern Empire and in England.

4. **Scandinavian activity** all over the Western world. Permanent settlement in Normandy begun. Progress in Russia. Attacks upon Constantinople. Explorations in the Far North.

5. Revived energies of Spanish Islam, which now approaches the zenith of its civilization.

Muhammadan pirates from Spain seize Fraxinetum on **888**
the coast of Provence, and from this lair ravage much of
S. France, W. Italy, even Switzerland, for a century—888
to 975. ['On one occasion Provençal Saracens and Magyars
from the Danube met at Orbe' near Lausanne, a few
miles north of the Lake of Geneva. 'It seemed as if the
enemies of Europe had met at her central point, and that
Christendom was doomed to succumb.']

Defeat of Scandinavians at Louvain.   **891**
Thus ends the last serious 'Danish' incursion into the
Middle kingdom or into Western Germany.

Fresh attacks of the Northmen (their chief leader the **894-7**
pirate Hasting) upon Wessex. Final victory of Ælfred.

Death of Ælfred. His reorganization of his kingdom, **901**
revival of the Militia, and creation of a Navy. His work
for civilization (learning, literature, &c.). The 'Anglo-
Saxon Chronicle'; Travels of Ohthere and Wulfstan;
Translations from Orosius' *Universal History*, Boethius'
Consolation of Philosophy, &c.; Asser's *Life of Ælfred*.

Eadward 'the Elder', son of Ælfred, renews the struggle **910**
with the Northmen, and begins the reconquest of the
Danelaw.

Fresh discovery of Greenland by the Northmen.   **c.910 (?)**

Extinction of the Frankish or Karling line in Germany **911**
(with the death of Lewis or Ludwig the Child, son of
Arnulf of Carinthia).

Foundation of Cluny, in Burgundy, which becomes the **912**
chief monastery of Roman Christendom. Thence beginning
of a powerful movement for Monastic and Church Reform,
associated with the highest ecclesiasticism ('School of
Hildebrand').

Permanent Scandinavian settlement and conquest in **911-22**
the North of France recognized by the cession of **Normandy**

(Northmen's Land) by the treaty of Clair-sur-Epte. The
invaders' leader, Hrolf ' the Ganger ' (Rollo the Rover),
an exile from Norway and Viking leader, baptized as
' Robert ', becomes the first Duke of Normandy (ancestor
of William the Conqueror). This treaty is probably in
part an imitation of the Wedmore arrangement [see 878].

912   Accession of Abdurrahman III in Spain (Amirat,
Sultanate, or Caliphate of Cordova). Revival of Muhammadan power in Spain under the ' Great Caliph ' (912–
61 ; ' Caliph ', formally, only from 929). Internal prosperity ;   magnificent buildings ;   science and learning.
The schools of Cordova, during all the tenth century,
a centre of the highest Western culture. Their Christian
pupils and influence on Christendom. Splendid Muslim
buildings in Spain : the Great Mosque at Cordova, founded
785, extended [see 929, 961, 990].

**c. 912–
920** Incessant Hungarian attacks upon German lands,
Italy, &c.

Weakness and misery of all the Christian countries of
the West (England a partial exception).

PERIOD XII

FROM THE ACCESSION OF HENRY THE FOWLER TO THE FOUNDATION OF THE HOLY ROMAN EMPIRE OF THE GERMAN NATION, 919–62

General Points

1. **Foundation of the great German state of the Middle Ages,** which lasts as the most powerful in Europe till fatally weakened in the thirteenth century.

Victories over enemies (Hungarians, Danes, &c.). Conquests from Slavs beyond Elbe. Internal consolidation.

Interference in Italy.

As result of this :

1 *a.* **Revival of the Western Empire,** under the German kings, as the **Holy Roman Empire of the German Nation.**

2. English revival in Britain. Scandinavian conquests [*Danelaw*, &c.] recovered by West Saxons under House of Ælfred. **Zenith of Anglo-Saxon state.**

3. **Spanish Islam** (Western Caliphate) **at the height of its power and** prosperity, both in politics and **civilization.**

4. Beginnings of fresh territorial advance of the Eastern Empire, largely as result of

5. Weakness and **decay of Eastern** [Baghdad] **Caliphate.**

6. Scandinavian activity. Complete formation of the *Norman* settlement in N. France.

919   **Henry the Fowler,** Duke of the Saxons, the true founder of the mediaeval German kingdom, *elected* German ('East Frankish') *king* (Henry I). *Troubled state of the German lands* at this time. All beyond the Elbe occupied by the Slavs. Germany proper (the 'East Frankish' land) is still really composed of separate states ('duchies') of Saxons, Franconians, Bavarians, Swabians, &c. Terrible sufferings from invasions of Scandinavians, Slavs, Hungarians, &c. Great part of Lotharingia occupied by France (the 'West Frankish' kingdom).

922   Complete re-conquest of the Midlands by Wessex (Eadward the Elder and his sister Æthelflaed).

924   First West-Saxon re-conquest of Northern England.

925   Henry the Fowler conquers Lotharingia from France.

926   Æthelstan (925–40) crushes movements of Scots, Welsh, and Scandinavians against the West Saxon Empire.

927   Henry the Fowler **begins the German eastward advance** (*Drang nach Osten*) at the expense of the Slavs. Conquests beyond the Elbe. Occupation of part of (the later) Brandenburg, from 927–8. The Mark of Brandenburg begun [see 936].
    First German Colonization beyond Middle Elbe—towards region of [later] Berlin.

929   Abdurrahman III assumes the title of Caliph in Spain. ['*The Western Caliphate*' *proper*, 929–1031.]

c. 931,   **Beginnings of the Polish nation,** with Gnesen (Gniezno)
&c.   as capital.

933   Great German victory over the Hungarians. German successes against Bohemians and Danes. Creation of a Danish *Mark* [see 936], in certain regions of Holstein and Schleswig, by Henry (934).

936   Death of *Henry the Fowler*. 'In him, as in Alfred, is summed up the national hero—conqueror, colonist, deliverer.'

His *successes* in promoting *internal unity*—(a real German
state now begins)—in repulsing *foreign enemies*, and in
extending the kingdom and the limits of the German *race*.
Progress of *town life*. (' Henry the City-Builder.') His
system of ' *Marks* ', ' Marches ', Frontier Provinces, or
' Border-Jurisdictions ', out of which Prussia, Austria, and
modern Saxony have largely grown : e. g. (1) Schleswig,
against the Danes ; (2) and (3) Meissen and Brandenburg,
against the Slavs ; (4) Austria, against Hungarians. Each
was a ' nucleus of defence and civilization round which new
conquests grouped themselves ' [Stubbs]. Foundation of
new *fortresses* and restoration of old (nuclei of towns).
Henry's son **Otto ' the Great '** (936–73) succeeds.

League against Wessex defeated in the battle of *Brunan-* **937**
burh (commemorated in *Song of Brunanburh*).

Zenith of the **West Saxon power in Britain** under Æthel- **937–55**
stan, Eadmund, and Eadred. Complete submission of the
Danelaw. Northumbria made an earldom. Dunstan's
political career begins *c.* 946.

Successful struggles of Otto the Great against internal **937–55**
disaffection and against foreign enemies, Hungarians,
Danes, Slavs, &c. *Progress of the German expansion.*
Final defeat of the Hungarians (battle of the Lechfeld,
955) ; end of their attacks on Germany and Italy. They
settle down in the Hungarian plain, develop settled order
and civilization ; later they join Roman Christendom [see
1000].

Accession of Eadgar, the last of the great West Saxon **959**
kings (959–75), under whom many symptoms of decay
are noticeable. Dunstan, Archbishop of Canterbury (959–
85), is the chief English statesman of this period.

Byzantine re-conquest of Crete (by Nikephoros Phokas). **960–1**
Crete, lost 823, had long been a terrible plague to the
Empire as a base of Muhammadan piracy and war.

Beginnings of the new Byzantine territorial recovery ('l'Épopée Byzantine ').

961   Otto's second expedition to Italy (first in 951) nominally to aid Pope John XII against his enemies. In Rome Otto *renews the Imperial office.*

962   Beginnings of the **Holy Roman Empire of the German Nation**—which lasts, as a vital factor in European history, till the Great Interregnum (1256–73) ; retains some value till the abdication of Charles V (1555), or even perhaps till the Peace of Westphalia (1648) ; and continues in name till 1806. Importance of this. Contrast with the Empire of Charles the Great (which is Germany *plus* France, *plus* Burgundy, *plus* Italy;—whereas the Holy Empire as finally constituted is Germany *plus* Italy—and later *plus* Burgundy, but never including France. The ' Ottonian restoration ' also is less ecclesiastical, and less ' Roman ' than the Carolingian ; but it was ' based on a social force which the other had wanted ' [Bryce].

PERIOD XIII

FROM THE RESTORATION OF THE EMPIRE BY OTTO THE GREAT TO THE CAPETIAN ERA IN FRANCE, 962–87

GENERAL POINTS

1. The **revived Western Empire under the German kings.** Its work in Italy. Crushing of movements towards Italian nationalism.

Imperial control of Papacy and of city of Rome asserted and maintained. First German reform of the Papacy.

2. **Advance of the Eastern Empire** at the expense of the Muhammadan world and of the Barbarians in the Balkans. Extensive conquests in Asia and Europe ('l'Épopée Byzantine ').

3. Extinction of the Carolingian line in France. Hugh Capet founds the new **Capet dynasty,** which continues (in various lines) till the end of monarchy in France (1848).

4 Continued power and **splendour of Spanish Islam** and its civilization. Deep influence of this on Western Christendom.

5. **Scandinavian activity.** Renewal of attacks on England.

Fresh Norse discoveries.

Attacks on the Eastern Empire. Colonization of Greenland begun.

6. **Progress of Christian missions** in the North and East of Europe, especially among Danes, Norwegians, Swedes, Russians, and Poles.

962–92   Mieczyslaw I, first King of Poland.

963–4   Otto causes the deposition of Pope John XII, and asserts the *Imperial* (German) *control over the Papacy*, which he reforms. The Roman clergy and people have to promise not to elect popes without the Imperial consent.

This *first German 'reformation of the Papacy'* is succeeded, after a time, by a fresh period of Papal degradation and dependence on local nobles.

963–9   Progress of the Byzantine revival. Nikephoros Phokas, co-emperor and regent. Fresh conquests (Cilicia, 964–5 ; Cyprus, 965 ; Antioch, 969; and other parts of North Syria, e.g. Aleppo, Emesa). No city of Syria remained so long in Christian hands as Antioch, retained by the Eastern Empire till 1081 ; recovered by the (First) Crusaders in 1098 ; finally lost to Islam, 1268.

965–7   The **Polish** King (Mieczyslaw) and his court embrace **Roman Christianity,** which becomes the national religion.

968   Embassy from the Western Empire to the Eastern, under Liudprand ('Luitprand'), Bishop of Cremona, one of the most interesting writers of the tenth century. Badly received at Constantinople, Liudprand roundly abuses everything, especially Nikephoros himself, 'in colour an Ethiopian ; bold of tongue, a fox by nature, in perjury and lying an Ulysses. . . .'

The Eastern Emperor, encouraged by success, haughtily refuses to barter away Byzantine (S.) Italy to Otto, and threatens war.

969   John Tzimiskes, Byzantine general, murders Nikephoros Phokas, and becomes co-emperor and regent in his place (969–76). 'Thus perished . . . a brave soldier, an able general . . . one of the most virtuous men and conscientious sovereigns that ever occupied the throne of Constantinople ' [Finlay].

Re-conquest of Eastern Bulgaria. Victorious war with **969–76**
the Russians (Svyatoslav defeated and forced to surrender
at Dorystolon on the Danube, 971). Revolts, recoveries,
and fresh conquests in Syria—advance into Mesopotamia.
Diarbakr or Amida, Edessa, Nisibis, Beirut captured,
973–5. Momentary recovery of Jerusalem (?).

Interview between Tzimiskes and Svyatosláv on the **969–76**
Danube, one of the most picturesque passages of mediaeval
history, as described by Leo the Deacon. The emperor's
' diminutive body endowed with the soul of an hero '
[Gibbon].

Death of Otto I. His ability, practical sense, untiring **973**
energy, conscientiousness, ubiquity. ' Constantly travers-
ing his dominions, he introduced peace and prosperity . . .
and left everywhere the impress of an heroic character.
Under him the Germans became united . . . raised on a
pinnacle . . . as the imperial race ' [Bryce].

Death of John Tzimiskes. Basil II, the ward and co- **976**
emperor of Nikephoros Phokas and John Tzimiskes (963–
76 ; cf. the last Frankish kings of the House of Clovis
and the Mayors of the Palace), now becomes real sovereign,
976–1025. His reign marks the *zenith* of the political and
military strength *of the Eastern Empire* (since Justinian),
' the culminating point of Byzantine greatness '.

[' Indefatigable, brave, and stern, Basil's courage degener-
ated into ferocity. . . . He believed . . . he was prudent,
just, and devout ; others considered him rapacious, cruel,
and bigoted. For . . . learning he cared little . . . he was
a type of the higher Byzantine moral character . . . more
. . . Roman than . . . Greek. In . . . military skill he had
few equals.'—Finlay.]

St. Mark's, Venice (the present church), commenced.   **977**

Al Mansur (' Almanzor '), the most successful military **978**
leader of Spanish Islam, becomes practical dictator of the

Caliphate of Cordova (978–1002). In 985 he takes Barcelona ; in 987 Leon.

Spanish Christendom again driven back into the mountain fastnesses (Asturias, Pyrenees).

980 *Scandinavian attacks*, mainly Danish, upon England recommence. They increase in force till the *great Danish conquest of England* is achieved (by 1014–16).

981 The Emperor Basil II (976–1025), ' Slayer of Bulgarians ' (' Boulgaroktonos '), begins the final Byzantine conquest of all Bulgaria (finished 1018).

983 The palace-church of Charles the Great at Aachen, ruined by the Northmen, is rebuilt. (Till 1531 this remains the regular place of the coronation of the German kings.)

983 Death of Otto II. Otto III, a child of three years old, succeeds. Partly as a result of this, a Pagan and anti-German reaction breaks out in the newly-won Slav lands beyond the Elbe. For over a century the German expansion is put back.

985 Eric the Red, exiled from Iceland, begins the Scandinavian colonization of Greenland.

987 Death of Louis *le Fainéant* (' Do-Nothing '), King of the West Franks or ' French '. Extinction of the direct line of Charles the Great. Hugh Capet, Duke of the French, Lord of Paris, chosen king (987–96). Writing at the opening of the fourteenth century, Dante views him as

> ' the source of that malignant plant,
> That overshadoweth now the Christian world
> So that good fruit is seldom gathered from it '.

The direct *Capetian line* lasts till 1328 (death of Charles the Fourth) ; in younger branches (Valois, Bourbon) till 1793 (and, after the Restoration of 1815, till 1848). Paris, the centre of the power of the House of Eudes (Counts

or Dukes of the French), tends to become the permanent
capital of the French monarchy.

Laon, the royal city of the Western Carolingians (the
Karling kings of France), gradually sinks into a small
provincial town.

Immense power of the great vassals in France, completely overshadowing the Crown under all the early
Capetians, as under the later Carolingians.

Not till Louis VI (1108–37) does the royal power
begin to make much headway. Philip II, ' Augustus '
(1180–1223), is the true creator of the great French
monarchy.

PERIOD XIV

FROM THE ACCESSION OF HUGH CAPET IN FRANCE TO THE BEGINNING OF THE ELEVENTH CENTURY, 987-1002

GENERAL POINTS

1. The **Western Empire and German Kingdom,** though harassed by difficulties in Italy, by a Pagan and anti-German reaction among the Slavs beyond the Elbe, and by the growth of the Polish power, **maintains its** premier **position** in W. Europe. Short-lived attempt (of Otto III) to revive the Roman Empire in a stricter sense, with Rome as the seat of government and imperial residence.

2. Continued **progress and prosperity of the Eastern Empire** [see previous section].

3. Continued **prosperity of the Western Caliphate** [Spanish Islam ; see previous section].

4. **Progress of Christian missions** in north and east of Europe. **Conversion of** the sovereigns, courts, and governing classes among all the **Scandinavian peoples** (Northmen, Danes, and Swedes) ; also among the **Russians,** the **Poles,** and the **Hungarians.**

5. **Zenith of Scandinavian activities.** Attacks on England. Colonization of Greenland. Discovery of North America. Intercourse with Constantinople.

6. **Formation of a powerful Polish state** [see (1) and (4) above].

7. **Power and prosperity of** the Slav-Scandinavian **Russians** [see (4) above].

8. The **Hungarian state takes permanent form.**

Progress of the Scandinavian colonization of Greenland, **987, &c.**
especially in extreme south.

Vladimir, the Russian Grand Prince (972–1015), accepts **c. 988**
Greek Christianity, which from this time gradually **becomes**
the **national faith of the Russian race.** (Some progress had
been made by Greek Church missions to the Russians as
early as 867.)
Russia is the chief gain of the Eastern Church in
history.

'Almanzor' completes the Great Mosque at Cordova, **990, &c.**
commenced in 785, and added to by successive Amirs and
Caliphs of the Umayyad dynasty in Spain,—'the largest
and most noble monument of the architecture of the
Spanish Arabs', and in many respects of Islam.

Scandinavian attacks on England increase in violence. **991**
Battle (and song) of Maldon.

Olaf, the 'Lap king', makes **Roman Christianity** the **993–**
national faith in Sweden.   **1024**

Otto III (born 980 ; German king from 983) crowned **996**
emperor. His dream of restoring Rome as the real capital
of the Western Empire.

Olaf Tryggveson, King of **Norway,** introduces **Roman 996–**
Christianity as the **national faith.**   **1000**

Boleslaw I, King of Poland, founder of **Polish greatness. 996–**
His vast conquests (Bohemia, Moravia, Silesia, Pomerania, **1025**
Old Prussia, part of Russia and of later Brandenburg, &c.).
Though much of this is only temporary, part is permanent,
and *henceforth Poland takes rank as an independent and*
important Christian power.

Olaf Tryggveson builds a royal residence and church **c. 996**
(the first cathedral of Norway) at Nidaros or Trondhjem,
which for a time becomes one of the leading court-towns
and capitals of Europe [see 1015, 1090].

990-7 Continued victories of Spanish Islam under ' Almanzor ' ; Galicia overrun ; Compostella taken. Spanish Christendom now apparently confined within narrower limits than at any time since the first Muhammadan conquest of Spain [711, &c.]. Deceptive character of much of this.

997- Stephen, first King of **Hungary** ['St. Stephen '], makes
1002, **Roman Christianity** the national faith, settles and organizes
&c. his people as a **nation** of Catholic **Europe** [997-1038], and takes the royal title [1001].

999 The great scholar and scientific pioneer, Gerbert, the confidant, tutor, and adviser of Otto III, once a pupil of the Muhammadan Spanish Schools, and long head of the Schools of Rheims, becomes Pope, as Sylvester II (999-1003).

997- The Turkish Sultan, Mahmud of Ghazni, begins the
1028 Muhammadan conquest of North India.

Before Carpets begin to be introduced again into W. Europe,
1000 especially from Muhammadan Spain.

1000 **Discovery of** some part of **North America** by the Scandinavians. Leif, son of Red Eric, returning to his home in S. Greenland (Eric's Fiord) from the court of Norway, is carried by stress of weather to *Vineland the Good* (Southern Nova Scotia, or some region not very far south of this).

1000 Death of King Olaf Tryggveson at the battle of Svold. Norway partitioned by Sweden, Denmark, and Norse rebels.

1000-2 Christian rally in Spain. ' Almanzor ' checked.

1002 Death of Al Mansur (' Almanzor '), and of Otto III, followed by that of Pope Sylvester II (1003).

Massacre of Danes in England, on St. Brice's Day (November 13). The Danish King, Swegen Fork-Beard, resolves on the conquest of England. Scandinavian attacks increase in force till the complete Danish conquest of 1014-16.

GENERAL VIEW OF THE STATE OF EUROPE ABOUT A.D. 1000

1. Civilization has received terrible shocks since **476** : has been in danger of at least partial paralysis : has not up to the end of the tenth century shown much promise of fresh life. The Revivals of Culture attempted (e.g. under Charles the Great) have not proved permanent.

But the revival of comparatively healthy social and political life is already beginning to be felt. After terrible struggles, European life has been in great measure regenerated by Germanic, Scandinavian, and other conquerors and settlers.

The Old, all-embracing, Empire has gone : but in its place we have the New Nations, already beginning to show highly developed political consciousness and energy.

The Old, all-prevailing, Western Language has gone, except for the special use of Churchmen. In its place are the New Languages, which in time will produce the New Literatures.

The Old Latin Literature has gone. In its place is the New Latin Literature of the Church, which since the fifth century (still more since the rise of Islam) has little literary pretension.

The Old Paganism, in all its varieties, has gone. In its place is the Christian Church, dominating, or deeply affecting, every important race of Europe, and nearly every phase of European life.

The Old Philosophy has gone. In its place is the beginning of the New Christian Philosophy (Scholasticism). The 'Theological interest' remains the most powerful of all intellectual forces.

The Old Social and Economic Conditions (Roman Slavery, Morality, Luxury, &c.) are profoundly changed or modified.

The Christian tendency towards the Emancipation of all the Unfree is already to be noticed.

The Old Culture, Wealth, and Refinements have gone. The New Christian society is comparatively poor, rough, hard-living, ignorant, unrefined. But with greater purity, virility, capacity, originality, and promise.

Knowledge of the world, in Christian Europe, has been greatly contracted in east, south-east, and south, since the days of the Old Empire, but on the other hand has been notably extended to north, north-east, and north-west.

Islamic civilization has reached perhaps its highest development, and has both injured and benefited Christendom deeply.

2. The **EAST ROMAN** or Byzantine **EMPIRE,** now entirely non-Latin, governed from Constantinople, still represents the Caesars, and is the lineal descendant of the realm of Constantine. It is now at the height of a long period of revived energy and power, though it has lost (since 800) even the formal allegiance of nearly all of Western Christendom.

3. Among the New Institutions and **NEW STATES** of Europe, the Roman **PAPACY** has established its ascendancy over nearly all parts of Western Christendom, and has definitely advanced a claim to a spiritual monarchy over the whole Christian world. This has helped to produce a permanent schism of Eastern and Western Christians: the 'Greeks' have (since the ninth century) clearly rejected the more extreme Papal claims. The Papacy is still normally submissive in secular matters to the civil power, especially as embodied in the new imperial authority it has done so much to create.

The New Western or **HOLY ROMAN EMPIRE** is also near the zenith of its real political development and success.

Originally founded as an almost Universal Dominion of
the West under the Frankish kings, largely through the
action of the Church of Rome, in revolt from the Eastern
Empire, it soon fell to pieces, in this larger and more unwieldy
form, but was revived in a smaller, more compact, and
manageable shape. It is now the 'Holy Roman Empire
of the German Nation', and is based entirely upon the
leading position of the Germanic people and kingdom in
Roman Christendom.

No other of the New **Western States,** France, England,
the Spanish kingdoms, the Italian Republics, &c., have
reached the same apparent prosperity and strength.
But the success of the Germans is prophetic of similar
developments in France, England, Spain, and Italy. In
Russia the Slav-Scandinavian principalities seem effectively federated under Kiev. Hungary, Norway, and Denmark appear as powerful and united realms.

The **conversion** of Hungary, Russia, and the Scandinavians at this time (or in the next few years) almost
completes Mediaeval Christendom both in east and west.
Only one important race (the Lithuanians) remains to be
added to Christian Europe.

SCANDINAVIAN activity is at its height. The expansion of the Scandinavian races now reaches from Greenland
and America to Russia, Constantinople, and Morocco.

PERIOD XV

FROM THE OPENING OF THE ELEVENTH CENTURY TO THE COMMENCEMENT OF THE HILDEBRANDINE PAPACY, 1002–48

GENERAL POINTS

1. The **Western Empire** (and German kingdom) at the **height of its power** and prosperity.

2. The **Revival of the Eastern Empire at its height.**

3. **Scandinavian activity at its zenith** (conquest of England ; beginning of dominion in S. Italy ; attempted American colonization ; development in Russia, &c.).

4. Continued **progress of Christian Missions** among northern races. **Christendom,** eastern and western, **attains its final extension in Europe, with slight exceptions** (Prussians, Lithuanians, &c., won in thirteenth–fourteenth centuries).

5. **Prominence of the Russians,** now converted to Greek Christianity, under the Grand Princes of Kiev.

6. Depression of the French kingdom.

7. **Collapse of the Western Caliphate** and disruption of Spanish Islam.

8. Beginnings of the **Turkish Age in Eastern Islam.** Turks masters of the Caliph in Baghdad.

9. Beginnings of the **Mediaeval Renaissance** in Western civilization. **Close of the Dark Ages** [even in ' Culture '. In Politics the new time of life and vigour in Christendom begins in the tenth century ; see above, 919, 962, &c.].

Struggles of the North African and other Muhammadans **1002–50**
with various Christian powers, especially Pisa and Genoa,
for the possession of Corsica and Sardinia, which are now
finally won back for Christendom. Sicily still held by
Islam.

Fresh developments of civilization and culture in Western
Europe. ' It was as if the world were awaking again '
(speaks a contemporary), ' as if it everywhere threw away
its old dress, and put on a white vesture of churches.'
And the churches of the eleventh century ' have a . . .
character of their own. It is no longer Roman art in
debasement, but a style fresh and vigorously original—
the solemn, massive, and enduring architecture ' which
marks the full development of ' Romanesque ', ' Lombard ',
or ' Norman '.

About this time we get the earliest certain important
examples of the art of staining glass (e. g. at Rheims).

About this time also there is marked progress in the
higher studies and thought of Western Christendom.

Expedition from Greenland, under Thorfinn Karlsefne, **1003–6**
to plant a *colony in Vineland* (*N. America*). It apparently
coasts the greater part of Nova Scotia ; attempts to settle
in the south of this region ; touches Southern Labrador
and Newfoundland. The colonial experiment fails (native
hostility ; quarrels of colonists over their women) and the
fleet returns to Greenland.

The (Romanesque) cathedral of Mainz completed. Begun **1009**
973, it underwent large additions in the twelfth–fourteenth
centuries, but remains one of the chief Romanesque buildings north of the Alps.

Hakim Biamrillah, a mad Fatimite Caliph, destroys the **1010**
Christian buildings at the Holy Sepulchre in Jerusalem.
This outrage helps the growth of the crusading spirit in
Roman Christendom.

The clan of the *Fatimids* or Fatimites, who claimed descent from Fatimah, the daughter of Muhammad, became the heads of the *Ismailian* heresy in Islam—an offshoot from the main body of *Shiite*, or non-orthodox Muhammadanism, which rejected the traditions (*Sunna*) and the regular line of Caliphs.

Ismailism gradually developed, as a vast secret society, in a frankly ' atheistic ' and ' Antinomian ' direction, rejecting all fixed rules of religion and morality—actions were indifferent, only the internal disposition mattered. It adopted an allegorical interpretation of the Kuran, by which any doctrine might be defended or rejected.

The Fatimite leaders founded an independent state in N. Africa, with a capital near Tunis, in 909—setting up a rival Caliphate, and extending their sway to Egypt in 969–72, and to Syria before the close of the tenth century. The sect of the *Assassins* was a later development of the same movement, from about 1090.

1014   Death of Swegen Fork-Beard of Denmark, after reconquering all the old *Danelaw* (North-East England) for the Scandinavian dominion.

His son Cnut (Knud, ' Canute ') succeeds him.

The English elect Eadmund Ironside. Desperate fighting between English and Danes.

1015   St. Olaf becomes King of *Norway* and reunites the country, settling *Christianity as the permanent national faith.*

After   St. Olaf rebuilds Trondhjem (*Nidaros*), now for some
1015   time the regular capital of Norway [see 996, 1090].

1016   Death of Eadmund Ironside. *All England submits to Cnut and the Danes.* Cnut the Great and his *Empire of the North* (Denmark and the English Danelaw, 1014 ; rest of England added, 1016 ; Norway, 1028).

As King of Norway, Cnut was also overlord of the various Norse possessions in the Ocean (Orkneys, Hebrides, Iceland, Greenland, &c.).

Reign of Yaroslav, ' the Great ', ' the Lawgiver ', as **1016-54** Grand Prince of Russia, in Kiev. Closer union of the *Russian Principalities under the suzerainty of Kiev.* The new *Russian civilization,* mainly derived from the Eastern Empire. The Russian political system long retained the old freedom, division of powers, weakness of organization. The Tartar Conquest caused (Moscovite) Russia to imitate Constantinople here also [see p. 172].

Basil II completes the *conquest of Bulgaria* for the **1018** Byzantine Empire (permanent till 1187).

Servia also incorporated. Imperial suzerainty over Croatia. The *Byzantine Revival at its height.*

Norman dominion in S. Italy begins with the *County of* **1018** *Aversa* (mainly the creation of bands of adventurers from Normandy).

Church and Hospital of St. John founded in Jerusalem **1020** by merchants of Amalfi. This is the germ of the later Order of the Hospitallers or Knights of St. John [see p. 97].

The prosperity and power of the *Republic of Amalfi is now at its height* (throughout eleventh century, to the Crusades).

Cathedral of St. Sophia, Kiev (still existing), built by **1020-37** the Grand Prince of the Russians, Yaroslav the Lawgiver. Remarkable work of Byzantine architecture and art in early Russia (churches, monasteries, palaces, frescoes, mosaics, &c.).

Death of the Emperor (and German King) Henry II **1024** (' the Saint ').

End of the Saxon Dynasty, which is succeeded by the Franconian or Salian (1024-1125).

1025   Death of Basil II of Constantinople. Immense extension of the Eastern Empire during his reign, both in Europe [see above] and in Asia, where great part of Armenia and Caucasia are annexed.

1027   Conrad II, the first Franconian Emperor, crowned at Rome (Cnut the Great present).

The Eyder made the boundary between Germany and Denmark (Schleswig, therefore, definitely assigned to the Danish sphere).

1028   St. Olaf of Norway expelled from his kingdom by an invasion of Cnut the Great and rebellion at home. He flies to Novgorod, reorganizes his party, and prepares for a restoration.

1030   St. Olaf of Norway, attempting to recover Norway, is defeated and slain at Stiklestad. He becomes the national saint, and by his ' martyrdom ', more than by his life, does much to win the day for Christianity in Scandinavia.

1031   **Break-up of the Western or Spanish Caliphate** (' of Cordova '). The small Moorish states, which result from this, are unable to stem the Christian revival and reconquest.

1030–2   Fresh struggles between Poland and Germany. Conrad wins Lusatia (in modern Saxony) for the Empire (1031), and compels the Polish king to do him momentary homage (1032).

c. 1030–   About this time, introduction of the *Truce of God*
1050   (*Truga* or *Treuga Dei*) in Guienne, whence it spreads to the rest of France, and to some other parts of Christendom. By this the Church endeavoured to enforce a truce to all feuds during Christian festivals, and from the Wednesday evening to Monday morning in every week.

1032–5   *Burgundy*, through the victorious campaigns of the Emperor Conrad II, is *united to the Empire*, which is thus extended to the Rhone valley, the Cevennes, and the coast of Provence, and includes Lyons, Marseilles, Geneva, Besançon, &c.

The Empire now (and till the fourteenth century) effectively made up of the *three kingdoms—Germany, Italy, Burgundy.*

Death of *Cnut the Great. Dissolution of his Empire* of the **1035** North (1035–42).

Reconquest of Eastern Sicily from Muhammadan rule **1038–42** by Byzantine armies under George Maniakes.

The Saljuk (' Seljuk ') Turks from Central Asia conquer **1039** the west of Persia, and begin to dominate the Eastern (Baghdad) Caliphate.

From that day to this **Turkish influence** and Turkish races have dominated the central lands of **Islam.**

Henry III (' the Black '), German King and Emperor.   **1039–59** The German kingdom is never more powerful than in this period (except perhaps under Otto I). Victory of the central government over internal rivals and difficulties.

Of the five great dukedoms, Henry keeps three in his own hands for a time.

Increase of pilgrimage to Palestine. [' At this time there **c. 1040,** began to flow towards the Holy Sepulchre so great a multi- **&c.** tude as . . . no man could have hoped for. First went the meaner folk, then men of middle rank, and lastly kings and counts, marquises and bishops ; aye, and . . . many women.'—Ralph Glaber.]

Partial revolt of Serbia from the Eastern Empire.   **1040**

The English Restoration. End of Danish rule. Reign **1042** of Edward the Confessor (1042–66).

The *Normans* form their County of *Apulia,* and begin **1042** to be the *dominant power in the extreme south of Italy.*

German war with Hungary. The Hungarian king **1042–4** becomes (momentarily) a vassal of the Empire.

Extension of the Bavarian *eastern march* (the *Oesterreich, Austria*) to the Leitha (still to-day the eastern frontier of the Austrian dominions proper, on the side of Hungary).

1046   Harald Hardrada becomes King of Norway (d. 1066, q.v.) after a life of romantic adventure, often in the service of Russian princes and Byzantine sovereigns. His projects of North Polar exploration.

1046   Henry III makes his first expedition to Rome, and carries through a fresh *German Reformation of the Papacy.* Three rival popes (including Gregory VI, the champion and favourite of the reforming party) are deposed in Synod at Rome, and a new (German) pontiff elected as Clement II (Suidger, Bishop of Bamberg). With Clement II begins the series of austere and high-minded popes which maintains the moral position of the Papacy till the death of Boniface VIII (from 1046 to 1303).

Clement crowns Henry Emperor at Rome.

c. 1047, &c.   Rebuilding of the cathedral of Trier (Treves)—in its original form dating from *c.* 370, perhaps the oldest church in NE. Gaul, or Germany, and one of the oldest beyond the Alps.

1048   On the Imperial appointment of Bruno, Bishop of Toul, as Pope (Leo IX), **Hildebrand** and others persuade the new pontiff to treat the imperial nomination as insufficient, to refer his election to the choice of the Roman clergy and people, and generally to adopt the principles of the highest Catholic school, as taught at Cluny. *Hildebrand becomes the chief adviser of the Popedom* from this time (1048) till he becomes pontiff himself as Gregory VII (1073).

Real but veiled *beginning of the struggle between the Church, led by the* **Hildebrandine Papacy,** *and the Civil power, especially as represented in the Empire.* The war is more openly declared by Gregory VII on his accession, but the conflict is clearly foreshadowed from 1048, and the period 1048–73 is marked by various advances of the Ecclesiastical power at the expense of the Secular.

Hildebrand, a Tuscan, probably of mixed Teutonic and native Italian stock, born about 1010 (or slightly later) ; a churchman (probably a monk) of the strictest school, first at Rome, then at Cluny ; chaplain to Pope Gregory VI [deposed by Henry III ; see 1046]. He accompanies Gregory VI on his retirement into Germany ; after the latter's death, 1048, again withdraws to Cluny.

Most original and creative of Papal statesmen, the extremest developments of Papal theory are due to his inspiration. ' Filled with magnificent visions of ecclesiastical grandeur, he pursued his designs with indomitable steadiness, . . . far-seeing patience, . . . deep, subtle, and unscrupulous policy. He well knew how to avail himself of small advantages towards more important ends, or to forego the lesser in hope of attaining the greater. He knew how to conciliate, . . . flatter, . . . threaten, and denounce. Himself impenetrable and inflexible, he was especially skilled in understanding . . . other men, and in using them as his instruments.']

PERIOD XVI

FROM THE BEGINNING OF THE HILDEBRANDINE REVIVAL OF THE PAPACY TO THE FIRST CRUSADE, 1048–96

GENERAL POINTS

1. **Development of the 'Hildebrandine' or 'Ultramontane' Papacy.** Attempt to realize a **Papal Monarchy over Western Christendom,** not only in matters spiritual, but also (to a large extent) in matters temporal.

2. Consequent **struggle of the Papacy and the Empire.** Temporary defeat and abasement of the Emperor. Partial Imperial Recovery.

3. Origin of the (Palestine) **crusading movement.** (Grievances of pilgrims. Danger of Eastern Empire, &c.)

4. **Scandinavian activity.** (*a*) Norman Conquest of England : Anglo-Norman dominion of William the Conqueror, the most powerful state west of the Empire. (*b*) Norman Conquest of South Italy and Sicily.

5. **Progress of Christendom in Spain :** partially checked by Muslim reinforcement from Africa ('Almoravide' Dominion).

6. **Progress of the Turks in Asia.** Their domination at Baghdad. Their victories over the Eastern Empire. Asia Minor overrun. Constantinople threatened.

7. **Progress of the 'Mediaeval Renaissance'.**
The new Christian culture and commerce.

Progress of the Commercial Cities of Europe, especially in Italy (Flanders, Germany, and Russia also).

Foundation of the *Order of the Hospital* or *of St. John* **1048**
of Jerusalem, the oldest of the three great Orders of Military
Monks (Hospitallers, Templars, Teutonic Knights).

But until the Crusades, and even until the foundation
of the Templars, the Hospitallers are mainly concerned
with the protection of pilgrims and the care of the sick
[see 1020, 1118]. As a military Order, the Hospital largely
copies the Temple.

Pope Leo IX visits Germany and France, and holds **1049**
a Council at Rheims. Evident increase of Papal authority
in the west. All parts of Western Christendom submissive.
At Rheims 'it was asked, under threat of anathema,
whether any acknowledged any other Primate of the
Church. The claim was admitted by a general silence',
and the Papal Headship was solemnly declared.

First attacks of the Saljuk Turks upon the Eastern **1050**
Empire.

Imperial palace at Goslar (near the Harz) founded by **c. 1050**
Henry III. (Goslar remains to this day one of the most
interesting monuments of Mediaeval Germany.)

The Norman influence becomes dominant at the Eng- **1050–1**
lish court (forecast of 'Norman Conquest'). Robert of
Jumièges Archbishop of Canterbury. Exile of Earl Godwine, head of the 'English party'.

Godwine returns. Exile of the Norman favourites. **1052**
The House of Godwine supreme at court.

End of Muhammadan domination in Corsica and Sardinia. **c. 1050–**
Genoa and Pisa gain control of the islands. **1055**

Death of Godwine. His son, Earl Harold, succeeds to **1053**
his power.

Pope Leo IX, defeated and taken prisoner by the Normans **1053**
at the battle of Civitella ('Civitate') in South Central
Italy, invests them with all they could conquer in Apulia,

Calabria, and Sicily, as a fief of the Papacy. ['Since this memorable transaction the Kingdom of Naples has remained over 700 years a fief of the Holy See.'—Gibbon.]

1053–4   *Final formal breach between the Greek and Roman Churches* —practically effected in ninth century [see 863–7].

1055   The *Turkish* (*Saljuk*) *Sultan*, Togrul Beg, frees the Caliph of Baghdad from a number of petty oppressors, and is *invested with the temporal power of the Caliphate.*

1056   Death of the Emperor Henry III.   His infant son, Henry IV, succeeds (born 1050).   His long, weak, and turbulent minority is disastrous to Germany : e. g. in
    (1) Promoting internal disunion and disloyalty;
    (2) Allowing external enemies, especially the Hildebrandine churchmen, to gather strength.

1058   Harald Hardrada founds Oslo or Opslo [Old Christiania]. After the Union of Kalmar this becomes the capital of Norway [see 1397].

1059   Important council of the Western Church at Rome (' Lateran Council of 1059 ').   New regulations for *elections to the Papacy* ; *elective power* now practically *vested in the* **cardinals.**   Implicit challenge to imperial control of Papal elections, which are to be made ' saving the honour of our beloved son Henry, now . . . King, and hereafter, if God permit, Emperor, as we have already granted to him—· and also of his successors, who shall have personally obtained this privilege from the Apostolic See '.

1059–85   Robert ' Guiscard ' (' Wiscard ', i. e. the ' Sagacious ' or ' Cunning '), Duke of the Normans in South Italy.   A great conqueror and statesman, worthy of comparison with William the Conqueror of England.

1060–91   The *Norman conquest of Sicily.*   End of Muhammadan domination in the island.

1061   Completion of (present) cathedral at Speyer [' Spires ']

on the Middle Rhine (one of the chief examples of Romanesque architecture in Central Europe).

Earl Harold's campaign in Wales.   **1063**

Commencement of the Cathedral of Pisa, one of the chief **1063**
works of mediaeval architecture in Italy.

Struggles in Germany among the great nobles and **1062–72**
prelates for the control of the boy-king, Henry IV.

Revolt of Northumbria from Earl Tostig, Harold's **1065**
brother, who is driven out and flies to Norway to ask help
of Harald Hardrada.

Edward the Confessor completes his (Norman) church **1065**
of Westminster Abbey. This becomes the coronation-
place of English sovereigns from 1066 (Harold and William).

Death of Edward ' the Confessor '. Harold elected as **1066**
his successor. **William,** Duke of Normandy, claims the
crown of England, alleging (1) a bequest of the Confessor's ;
(2) an oath of Harold himself, when shipwrecked on
the Norman coast, and in William's power, about 1064 ;
(3) the right of his wife, Matilda of Flanders, a descendant of King Ælfred, through his youngest daughter
Ælfthryth.
William's claim is rejected, and he gathers a great army
to enforce it by conquest. The Papal blessing, through
the influence of Hildebrand, is given to his enterprise,
which thus takes something of the character of a crusade.

A Norwegian fleet and army, under Harald Hardrada, **1066**
bring Tostig back to Northumbria. The Norse invasion
of Yorkshire, undertaken with reckless daring and insufficient force, is repulsed by Harold of England at
Stamford Bridge (September 25, 1066). Death of Harald
Hardrada. [' A masterful man, given to rule in his land ;
sage of wit . . . no lord ever was in Northern Lands so
deep-witted, or so nimble of counsel' (hence *Hardrada*).

'A mighty warrior, and the boldest under weapons, strong and more skilled in arms than any other.'—*Harald's Saga.*]

1066   William of Normandy lands with his army at Pevensey. Harold hastens south, and fortifies the hill of Battle ('Senlac'), near Hastings. In the decisive **Battle of Hastings** (October 14, 1066), Harold is killed, with his brothers Gyrth and Leofwin, and his army cut to pieces. London and all South-Eastern **England submit** to William, who is crowned king at Westminster, Christmas, 1066.

1066, &c.   St. Stephen and the Trinity, at Caen (the churches of the Abbaye-aux-Hommes and the Abbaye-aux-Dames), begun by William the Conqueror and his wife Matilda.
Great age of Norman architecture (till near middle of twelfth century).

1067   The Saljuk Turks fiercely resume their attacks upon the Eastern Empire. They are checked, momentarily, by the Byzantine armies under the Emperor Romanos Diogenes.

1067–70   Castle of the Wartburg in Thuringia (Luther's refuge, 1521–2) built.

1067–71   *English risings against Norman rule, crushed* in detail (first in south-east, then in west, next in north, finally in the Isle of Ely and the Fen country : the great Norman *Wasting of the North,* 1069–70).

c. 1070–1075   Bergen founded by Olaf Kyrre, King of Norway.

1071   The *Saljuk Turks gain a decisive victory over the Byzantines* at **Manzikert** in Armenia. The Emperor is taken prisoner. The Turks ravage Asia Minor from end to end, and begin to form permanent settlements therein. From this time *Asia Minor* gradually becomes, as it still is, the *chief western home of the Turkish race.* The line of the Saljuk Sultans of *Rum* [i.e. would-be lords of the Eastern *Rome*], first reigning at Nicaea, then at Iconium, and aiming at Constantinople, begins 1081.

St. Mark's Church, Venice, completed. (This finest **1071**
example of Byzantine architecture in Western Europe was
begun 977.)

Final end of the Byzantine dominion in Italy. (Sur- **1071**
render of Bari to the Normans, April 1071.)

Hildebrand becomes Pope, as Gregory VII (April). The **1073**
High Catholic principles are now enforced more rigorously
than ever ; e.g. (1) total suppression of the marriage of
the clergy (*Nicolaism* and *clerical concubinage* in Hildebrandine language) ; (2) total suppression of *Simony,*
extended to mean, not merely the purchase of spiritual
office, but the obtaining of such office by any kind of
secular service ; (3) total suppression of *lay investiture,*
i.e. the bestowal of secular property and privileges upon
the clergy (and especially the symbols of high spiritual
office—ring and pastoral staff) by the temporal power,
whether a sovereign prince or an inferior lord.

Revolt of the Saxons against Henry IV.   **1073**

Gregory VII plans a *crusade,* or holy war of Christendom **1073-4**
against Islam, (*a*) to recover the holy places of Palestine,
(*b*) to save the Eastern Empire from the Turks.

Victory of Henry IV over the Saxons in the battle on **1075**
the Unstrut (in Thuringia). But the opposition to the
young emperor in Germany remains powerful, and gains
the upper hand when Henry's quarrel with the Church
comes to a head.

Open **quarrel between the Empire and the Papacy.** **1075-6**
Henry IV, threatened by Gregory with excommunication
and deposition (December 1075), declares Gregory deposed,
at the Council of Worms (January 1076). The German
bishops assent to this. **Excommunication and deposition
of Henry by Gregory** in synod at Rome, February 1076.
A German Diet at Tribur, October 1076, assents to the
excommunication of Henry, and suspends him from his

royal office, pending release from the Papal sentence and the favourable decision of the final Diet to be held at Augsburg in February 1077.

c. 1075   The *Bayeux tapestry* completed (a great strip of linen worked in coloured worsted with fifty-eight scenes from the life of William the Conqueror and the conquest of England, perhaps, as the tradition asserts, by Queen Matilda, William's wife).

1077   Henry IV goes into Italy, presents himself before the Pope at the Castle of **Canossa,** in the Apennines, makes abject *submission*, and obtains a conditional Papal absolution (January 25–28). For three days he is refused admission to the presence of Gregory, and compelled to wait as a suppliant in the snow-covered court of the castle.

1077   The rebel party in Germany elect, as anti-king, Rudolf of Swabia (in Diet at Forchheim).

1077, &c.   Rochester Cathedral and Castle (magnificent example of Norman fortress) built.

1078, &c.   Building of the original Tower of London (the *White Tower*) by William the Conqueror.

1079   Winchester Cathedral (the Norman church) commenced (great part finished 1093 ; largely rebuilt in Perpendicular style from *c.* 1360).

1080   Gregory proceeds to a second excommunication and deposition of Henry IV and to more stringent decrees against lay investiture (March). Henry and his party reply with the election of an anti-Pope, Wibert of Ravenna.

c. 1080   St. Alban's Abbey Church (the Norman building) completed.

c. 1080, &c.   Colchester Castle, with the largest Norman ' keep ' in England, erected (largely with Roman materials).

1080   Rudolf of Swabia, though victorious, is mortally wounded in a battle on the Elster.

Swabia given to Frederic of Hohenstaufen [see 1138, &c.], son-in-law of Henry IV.

Re-capture of Antioch by the Muhammadans (Turkish **1081** conquest). See 635, 969, 1098, 1268.

The (present) Cathedral of Mainz commenced. It **c. 1081** embodies part of the former church, mostly destroyed by fire 1009, restored 1036 and again burnt in 1081. ' The grandest monuments of the earlier mediaeval art in Germany are the Central Rhenish Romanesque cathedrals of Mainz, Speyer, and Worms.'

Robert Guiscard, at the head of the Norman power in **1081** S. Italy, attacks the Eastern Empire (with the probable ambition of seizing the throne of Constantinople and planting a Norman ' Latin ' Empire of the East in place of the Byzantine).

The Normans (under Guiscard) defeat the Byzantines (under the Emperor Alexios Komnenos) outside Durazzo (Dyrrhachium) and

Take Durazzo and march upon Constantinople. Their **1082** victorious advance is checked by the danger and appeals of Pope Gregory (their feudal suzerain) and by the fear of a German-imperial domination in Italy.

Henry IV comes down into Italy with a large force ; **1081–4** twice attacks Rome without success (1081–2) ; at last takes the greater part of the city (1083) ; has Wibert consecrated as Clement III (March 1084), and is himself crowned emperor by Clement (Easter 1084). All this time (1083–4) Gregory holds out in the Castle of St. Angelo, calling the Normans of Italy to his aid.

The Norman Cathedral of St. Paul's, London, begun.   **1083**

Robert Guiscard advances upon Rome, frees Pope **1084** Gregory (Henry IV retiring over the Alps), and sacks the city, inflicting terrible injuries (May–June 1084). Gregory leaves Rome, for good, with the Norman army. (Ancient monuments of Rome suffered especially at this crisis.)

1084   *Foundation of the Carthusian Order* at the Chartreuse, near Grenoble, by Bruno. This Order of Reformed Benedictine monks marks the second of the monastic revivals of the West—Cluny leading the first, the Cistercian Order the third [see 912, 1098].

Robert Guiscard resumes his attacks upon the Eastern Empire, defeating the Greek and Venetian fleets, and raising the siege of Corfu.

1085   Gregory VII dies at Salerno (May 25). (' Dilexi iustitiam et odi iniquitatem, propterea morior in exilio ')—' a second Athanasius, in a more fortunate age of the Church ' [Gibbon].

1085   Death of Robert Guiscard, chief creator of the Norman power in Italy (July 17). ' In less than three years ' he had delivered the Pope, and compelled ' the Emperors of East and West to fly before ' him [Gibbon].

> Sic uno tempore victi
> Sunt terrae Domini duo : rex Alemannicus iste,
> Imperii rector Romani maximus ille.
> Alter ad arma ruens armis superatur ; et alter
> Nominis auditi sola formidine cessit.
> [William of Apulia.]

His life is a picture of Scandinavian capacity in war and peace.

1085   **Hildebrandine principles** as summarized in the *Dictatus Papae* : e. g. ' That the Roman Pontiff alone can be rightly called *Universal* ; . . . that his name is unique in the world ; . . . that no General Synod [Council of the Church] can be called without his command ; . . . that his sentence can be annulled by no one ; that he alone can annul the sentences of all ; that he can be judged of no one ; that no one may dare to condemn one who has appealed to the

Apostolic Seat ; . . . that with his permission and by his command subjects may bring accusations [against their rulers] ; . . . that he can absolve subjects from their faith to the Unjust ; . . . that he can [lawfully] depose Emperors ; . . . that all princes shall kiss the feet of the Pope alone ; . . . that the Roman Church has never erred and will never err, the Scripture being witness ; . . . that no one may be accounted Catholic, who does not agree with the Roman Church '.

Alfonso VI of Castile and Leon permanently *recovers* **1085** *the old Christian capital of Toledo.* His raids to the Ocean and Mediterranean. Danger of Spanish Islam. To avoid complete political extinction, the Muslims of Andalusia call in the African (Moorish) ' Almoravides ', the warlike followers of the *Marabut* or ' Preacher '. ' Better be a camel-driver in Africa than a swine-herd in Castile.'

William the Conqueror orders a general survey of all **1085–6** England and of the possessions of all his subjects in Eng- land (the **Domesday Survey**). The result of the survey is *Domesday Book* (1086). ' So . . . narrowly did he cause the survey to be made that there was not a . . . rood of land, nor an ox, nor a cow, nor a pig passed by, that was not set down in the accounts—it is shame to tell what he thought no shame to do ' [*Anglo-Saxon Chronicle,* A. D. 1085].

At a special Great Court at **Salisbury,** William convenes ' all the landholding men of substance in England whose- soever vassals they were, and exacts a direct **oath** of allegiance from them, that they would be faithful to him against all others '. Thus he breaks through the inter- mediate feudal ties to inferior lords, and checks the growth of ' feudalism in government ', which had already proved so disastrous in France and so dangerous in Germany.

The Christian advance in Spain is checked by the great **1086** battle of Zalakka (Sacralias). But Toledo and the heart of the Peninsula are retained by Castile-Leon.

Before 1087 Buildings of William the Conqueror at the royal castle of Windsor. (Earlier buildings existed here, with a wooden enclosing stockade, under the later Anglo-Saxon kings.)

1087 Death of William the Conqueror, and temporary division of his empire among his sons : accession of William the Red [Rufus] in England, of Robert in Normandy.

' This King William . . . was a very wise and great man, more honoured and powerful than any of his predecessors . . . mild to those good men who loved God, but stark beyond measure towards those who withstood his will . . . very stern and wrathful, so that none durst do anything against his will. He imprisoned those earls who acted against his pleasure. He removed bishops . . . and abbots . . . he imprisoned thanes . . . he spared not his own brother.

' The good order . . . William established . . . was such that any man who was himself aught, might travel over the kingdom with a bosom-full of gold unmolested ; and no man durst kill another. . . . He was given to avarice, and greedily loved gain. . . . He loved the high deer as if he were their father. . . . The rich complained, and the poor murmured, but he . . . recked nought of them ; they must will all the king willed, if they would live.'

c. 1088 Beginnings of the **University of Bologna,** the earliest of the great permanent European centres of higher learning.

1088 Death of Lambert of Hersfeld, German historian.

c. 1088– 1095 The idea of a **crusade,** to free Palestine and especially Jerusalem from infidel rule, and to restore them to Christendom, almost brought to a head by Gregory VII in 1073–4, is revived by Pope Urban II, a disciple of Hildebrand (1088–99), and preached far and wide by the hermit Peter of Amiens, and others. The grievances of Christian pilgrims in Syria had largely increased since the Saljuk

Turks had become masters. The danger of Constantinople in particular, and of Eastern Christendom in general, specially appealed to Gregory VII, and was of great force in 1088–96. But the primary cause was in the fresh vigour and expansive energy of Western Christendom, seeking an outlet. The master-mind which finally organized the First Crusade was that of Urban.

Commencement of the great church of the Abbey of **1089** Cluny in its final form. When completed in 1311, it became, until the erection of the new St. Peter's at Rome, the largest church in Christendom. It was ruined at the French Revolution.

Beginning of Trondhjem Cathedral, ' still the finest **c. 1090** ecclesiastical edifice in Norway ' (though the Gothic nave is now utterly ruined), and for centuries the place of coronation of the Norwegian sovereigns [see 996, 1015].

The first (Norman) Cathedral of Lincoln completed **1092** (begun 1074).

Durham Cathedral (the present Norman church, the finest **1093** example of this style in England) begun.

Crusade Council at Clermont-Ferrand in Auvergne (1095). **1095** Great concourse, representative of both the clergy and laity of Christendom, Urban II presiding. The Pope's address and appeal. Passionate enthusiasm of the response : ' It is the will of God ' (*Deus vult*). Similar response throughout great part of Roman Christendom. Preparations for the crusade.

PERIOD XVII

FROM THE BEGINNING OF THE SYRIAN CRUSADES TO THE CONCORDAT OF WORMS, 1096–1122

GENERAL POINTS

1. **Opening of the crusading movement** in the Levant with fair success. **Conquest of** Jerusalem, Antioch, and great part of **Palestine and Syria.** Beginnings of **new Oriental influence upon Europe.**

2. **Beginning of the Orders of Knighthood** as fully-developed military and monastic brotherhoods, primarily to defend the crusading conquests in Syria.

3. Partial revival of the Eastern Empire, through the relief afforded by the First Crusade.

4. Rising importance of the **Italian** (and other South European) **commercial cities**; another consequence (in part) of the crusading movement.

5. **Truce in the struggle** between Empire and Papacy (and **between Spiritual and Civil Power,** generally, in W. Europe).

The Syrian Crusades (1076–1270) are the most important enterprises of Christendom as a whole in the Middle Ages or in modern times (as after the thirteenth century we do not find Christendom acting collectively, to any great extent—but only, as a rule, by nations). They end, in the thirteenth century, in political and military failure ; but their indirect effects are of the deepest and most permanent character. In a great measure they civilize Roman Christendom, introducing to it the culture, refinement, and luxury, and helping it to share in the wealth, of the East. A new Free Thought, and a new interest in and study of Nature, are among the chief results of the earlier Crusades. Effective movements of Syrian Crusade end with the close of the Twelfth Century [see 1190–1, 1202–4].

Start of the **First Crusade.**   1096

Various ' unofficial ', ill-organized, and ineffective bands of Crusaders start before the real army is ready. But the latter is composed of five distinct bodies, numbering in all perhaps 250,000 men, who march by different routes to Constantinople, where they unite and march across Asia Minor to North Syria. The leaders are :

1. Godfrey ' of Bouillon ', Duke of Lower Lotharingia, first ruler of the new Crusading State of Jerusalem.
2. His brother Baldwin of Boulogne, afterwards Lord of Edessa (1098–1100) and King of Jerusalem (1100–18).
3. Bohemund of Tarentum, son of Robert Guiscard ; with whom went
4. Tancred, Bohemund's cousin, afterwards Lord of Antioch.
5. Raymond, Count of Toulouse.
6. Bishop Adhemar of Puy, Papal Legate.

7. Robert of Normandy, son of William the Conqueror ;
with whom went

8. Stephen, Count of Blois ; and

9. Robert of Flanders.

The various bodies having united in the neighbourhood
of Constantinople, most of the leaders take an oath of
fealty to the (Byzantine) Emperor Alexios Komnenos,
promising to hold their conquests in fief of the Empire.

1097   They then help to besiege and take Nicaea (Nikaia,
' Nice '), the capital of the Saljuk Sultan of *Rum*, and
make it over to Alexios.   Thence they march overland to
Antioch, suffering much from Turkish attacks in the
upland of Asia Minor, but saving themselves in the battle
of Dorylaeum (July 1, 1097).

1097-8   Arrived before *Antioch*, they besiege the city for nine
months and *take* it in the early summer of 1098.   Great
Muhammadan attempt at recovery, under Kerboga, Amir
of Mosul (Nineveh), repulsed (June 28, 1098).

Antioch given as a principality to Bohemund.   No
leading Syrian city was so long in Christian hands.
Taken by the Muhammadans in 635, it was recovered by
Nikephoros Phokas in 969, and retained by the Eastern
Empire till 1084.   It was held by the Crusaders from 1098
to 1269.

1098   Meanwhile Baldwin, turning farther east, crosses the
Euphrates after the capture of Tarsus, *takes Edessa*, and
founds there (Easter, 1098) the most northerly, most
outlying, and most short-lived of crusading principalities
(lost 1144).

1098   Foundation of the **Cistercian Order,** under Robert, Abbot
of Molesme, at Citeaux in Burgundy [see 912, 1084].   St.
Bernard of Clairvaux, though not the founder, soon
becomes practical Chief of the Order [see 1115, &c.].

Siege and *storm of Jerusalem* (June 6—July 15). Terrible **1099**
massacre by the Crusaders.

Election of Godfrey of Bouillon as sovereign of the
new crusading kingdom ('of Jerusalem ').

He refuses the title of king, and rules as *Baron of the
Holy Sepulchre* (1099–1100). Baldwin I, his brother,
succeeds as king (1100).

Possible, but doubtful, reference to the use of the magnet **1099**
in navigation by an Italian versifying chronicler (William
of Apulia, in his *De Rebus Normannorum*).

Establishment of a *perfect Feudal organization in the new* **From**
Crusading States of the East : a kingdom (of Jerusalem) **1100**
with vassal counties (Antioch and Edessa ; with Tripolis
from 1109).

Building of Westminster Hall, and rebuilding of Old **1097–**
London Bridge, about this time. **1100**

The Tower of London area walled round.

Accession of Henry I of England. He issues a Charter **1100**
forbidding the exactions and abuses practised under William II, and restoring the 'law of Edward the Confessor'.

Accession of Baldwin I, first King of Jerusalem.

Zenith of crusading prosperity in the Levant.

The first cathedral at (old) Upsala commenced. **c. 1100**

Upsala had been the religious centre of heathen Sweden,
and it took the same place in Christian times. It was
also one of the chief royal residences; but till the fourteenth
century Sweden had no regular fixed capital (after the
French and English manner) ; then Stockholm took the
position.

Power of Hungary about this time. Prosperous reigns **c. 1100,**
of Ladislaus I (1077–95) and Koloman (1095–1114); con- **&c.**
quest of Croatia, part of Galicia, and Dalmatia (1102), the
last giving Hungary an extensive seaboard on the Adriatic,
and depressing the power and influence of Venice.

c. 1100, &c. Great increase of pilgrimage to Syria.

The ' war of the investitures ' is extended to England.

1103 Struggle between Henry I and Archbishop Anselm (1103–6).

1105 Death of the Emperor Henry IV. Henry V succeeds. ' If his sins were great, few men have borne heavier punishment than Henry IV.' His fifty years' reign, ' almost unparalleled in . . . Europe for its length of wretchedness ' [Stubbs]. [See 1075–7, 1080–4, &c.]

1106 Henry of England crushes the party of his brother Robert and masters Normandy (battle of Tinchebrai). *Restoration of the Anglo-Norman Empire.*

1107 The investiture quarrel settled in England [see 1122], by agreement between Henry I and Archbishop Anselm.

1108 Accession of Louis VI of France (1108–37), under whom the royal power at last begins to increase, mainly through the work of the chief French statesman of this time. Abbot Suger of St. Denys.

1109–10 The Leaning Towers at Bologna (' Asinelli ' and ' Garisanda ') completed.

1111 Death of Anselm, Archbishop of Canterbury (b. 1033 at or near Aosta, in Italy), one of the leading mediaeval saints, thinkers, and churchmen—' the first scholastic philosopher ' [not reckoning John Scotus Erigena among the Schoolmen ; see 877]. His ' ontological proof ' of the existence of God. Anselm's philosophical value not fully appreciated in the Middle Ages. His speculations have an originality and force greatly beyond the average of even the better *Scholastic* work.

1111 Momentary triumph of the Empire over the Papacy. Henry V occupies Rome, makes captive Pope Paschal II, and forces him to perform the imperial coronation, and to acknowledge the imperial right of investiture. These acts and concessions are repudiated on the retirement of the Emperor, by a Roman (Lateran) Council

The old Cathedral of Laon burnt. The present church **1112** is begun soon after this.

St. Bernard, the Cistercian, founds the Abbey of Clair- **1115** vaux [see 1098].

Foundation of the Order of the Temple (of Solomon), the **1118** most famous, and for a time the most popular and important of the Orders of Military Monks who play so great a part in the Middle Ages. The first Templars are nine French knights, who take Hugh de Payens, the first Grand Master (1118–36), for their leader [see 1048].

Completion of Pisa Cathedral (begun 1063).   **1118**

Commencement of the (present) Cathedral of Chartres, **c. 1120** one of the most splendid examples of mediaeval archi- tecture [see 1194].

The struggle of the Empire and the Papacy temporarily **1122** closed by the **Concordat of Worms,** which marks on the whole a *balance of success for the Secular Power.*

(i) In Germany [as in England ; see 1107] the civil power gives up, in name, the claim to appoint bishops and abbots. The cathedral chapter (or monastic body) is to elect the bishop ; the monks of the abbey are to elect the abbot ; but the election is to take place in the presence of the Emperor, or his representative. *Formal investiture by the Emperor* is abandoned, but the prelate-elect is to receive from the Emperor ' the property and immunities of his office', not with ring and staff, but with sceptre. *Bishops and abbots* were ' *to render* the *homage* which was the sign of their readiness to employ their temporal wealth and power on behalf of the State '.

(ii) In Italy and Burgundy much the same compromise is made, but here ' let the prelate receive his regalia six months after consecration '.

PERIOD XVIII

FROM THE CONCORDAT OF WORMS TO THE MIDDLE OF THE TWELFTH CENTURY, 1122–54

GENERAL POINTS

1. **Fresh Monastic Revival,** led by the Cistercians, in the Western Church.

2. **Revived strength of the German kingdom** and the Empire.
German expansion beyond the Elbe.

3. First signs of **increased power in the French kingdom.**

4. Formation of the **Anglo-Angevin Empire,** ending an orgy of feudal anarchy in England.

5. Beginning of the **kingdom of Portugal.**

6. Commercial and Social Developments. Growing **prosperity of trading cities,** especially in Italy.

7. Intellectual Developments.
Advances of **Scholasticism.**
The **New Western Literatures. New critical spirit.**
Struggles of Orthodoxy and Free Thought.

Death of Roscelin, a leading Schoolman, teacher of **c. 1122**
Abelard, and one of the founders of *Nominalism*.

Lincoln Cathedral rebuilding begun [see 1092,1147].   **1123**

Otto of Bamberg, 'Apostle of Pomerania', preaches **1124,**
among the Slavonic Wends of the South Baltic country.   **1127**

The *Order of the Hospital* (*of St. John of Jerusalem*) **1131**
transformed into an Order of Military Monks on the
pattern of the Templars [see 1020, 1048, 1118].

The 'Jews' House' and 'John of Gaunt's Stables' at **c. 1130–**
Lincoln, and 'School of Pythagoras' at Cambridge, some **1140**
of the oldest specimens of domestic [non-baronial] architecture in England.
The hall of Oakham Castle also belongs to about this
time.

Lothair of Saxony (German king, 1125–37) makes his **1132**
first expedition to Rome and is crowned emperor by Pope
Innocent II.

Fresh advances of **German** *conquest,* **colonization,** *and* **1125–34**
proselytism **beyond the Elbe.**   Many Slav [Wendish] tribes
submit and accept Christianity : others destroyed.
Since about 983 [which see] German progress beyond
the Elbe has been checked by Slavonic and heathen
revival.
The Altmark, &c., granted to Albert the Bear (1134),
who conquers the whole region of (later) Berlin.   This
region now begins to be known as *Brandenburg,* after its
chief township.   The Mark of Meissen, farther south (near
Dresden), granted to Conrad of Wettin.   Defeat of the
Danes : Holstein granted to Adolf, Count of Schauenburg.

Completion of the (Norman) Cathedral of Canterbury **1130**
(begun 1070, and almost entirely converted into Gothic
after 1174).

1130-50   The Norman *Roger II*, King of Sicily, makes his court one of the chief centres of civilization in Europe. His encouragement of Literature and Natural Science. Blend of Christian and Muhammadan culture in his dominions. Idrisi ('Edrisi') compiles his Arabic Geography at the court of Sicily, and dedicates it to Roger. Architecture in the Norman-Italian state. Roger defeated by the Emperor Lothair and temporarily driven from the Italian mainland into Sicily.

1134-48   Malachi, Bishop of Armagh (and Down), a friend of St. Bernard, works for the union of the Irish Church with Rome (completed by 1152).

1137   Death of Louis VI of France, under whom royal power had begun to grow [see 1108]. First signs of the future greatness of the French monarchy. Accession of the devout and weak Louis VII [1137–80].

1138-53   Civil War and Anarchy in England; parties of Stephen and Matilda. Practical loss of Northumberland and Cumberland to the Scots. Battle of the Standard, or Northallerton, 1138. Scottish invasion of Yorkshire thrown back.

1138-   *The House of Hohenstaufen* in Germany ('Die Staufer')
1254   named after the Castle of Staufen in Swabia (now in SW. Bavaria, about thirteen miles NW. of Sonthofen).

1138-52   Conrad III, first of the Hohenstaufen, elected by the Anti-Saxon party. Desperate struggle with Saxons and Bavarians. The Anti- and Pro-Staufer parties now become known as *Guelf* and *Ghibelline*, after *Welf* of the reigning House of Bavaria, and *Waiblingen*, a Hohenstaufen castle in Württemberg, about 7½ miles ENE. of Stuttgart. (*Guelf* and *Ghibelline* are Italian corruptions of these names. They became party war-cries, to denote Papalists and Imperialists, from the thirteenth century to the end of the fifteenth.)

St. **Bernard** *of Clairvaux,* the great leader of the Cis- **1138**
tercian Revival in Monastic Life, ends a Schism in the
Papacy : *his influence* dominant at the Papal court and in
Roman Christendom, 1138-53. 'The chief representative
of the strongest feelings of his age, the model of the
character it most revered, he found himself elevated to
such influence as no ecclesiastic, before or since, has '
surpassed [Robertson].

Progress of Portugal. Victory of Ourique over the Moors. **1139**
Count Affonso Henriques, the victor, declares himself king.
The **new Portuguese kingdom** does not yet include Lisbon
nor extend quite to the Tagus.

Bernard's controversies with Peter **Abelard** (Abailard),   **c. 1130-**
the champion of the **New Thought.** Abelard's work in the   **1142**
Schools of Paris from *c.* 1100.

Arnold of Brescia, pupil of Abelard, prominent as a critic   **c. 1140,**
of the Church.   **&c.**

Norwich Cathedral completed (begun 1096) : after **1140**
Durham this ranks first among the Norman churches of
England.

The *Nibelungenlied,* the chief work of German poetry of **c. 1140**
the early or ' heroic ' period, takes final form.

Completion (in great part) of the Abbey Church of St. **1140-4**
Denys, near Paris, in its present form, by Abbot Suger, the
chief adviser of the French kings Louis VI and Louis VII
in the middle of the twelfth century. Frankish kings had
been buried in the earlier church on this site from 638 :
Abbot Suger's church is the burial-place of the French
kings of the succeeding centuries. It is a typical example
of Romanesque developing into Gothic.

Death of Abelard, 'the founder of Modern Criticism ', **1142**
the first great modern champion of a ' moderate rationalism ',
greatest of university teachers of the twelfth century,
one of the first important names in French Literature.

Mainly through him, Paris becomes ' the hearth where
the intellectual bread of the whole World is baked '.
(Twenty of his pupils said to have become cardinals ;
fifty, bishops.)

1143-80   Manuel Komnenos, the last powerful Byzantine emperor,
' the first man among Christians ' (to his admirers).

1144   *Recapture of Edessa* by the Muhammadans under Imad-
ud-Din Zangi, Atabeg of Mosul, the first restorer of
Muslim power in the Levant after the crusading conquests
of 1097-1130.   The fall of Edessa is the immediate cause
of the next Crusade, which is preached, especially by
St. Bernard of Clairvaux, in the next years.

1144,   Imperial palace at Gelnhausen, in the Rhineland, built
&c.   (additions 1190-1200).

1147-9   **Second Crusade,** led by the Emperor Conrad III of
Germany and Louis VII of France.

The main armies march by the overland route, through
Hungary and the Balkan Peninsula, to Asia Minor.
Here the German army suffers severely :   part returns
home.   Most of the remainder, marching on overland to
Cilicia, are destroyed.   Conrad finally makes his way (like
Louis VII and the French nobles) by sea to the Holy
Land.   The Crusade ends in complete failure (futile attempt
on Damascus).   Frederick of Swabia, the future Emperor
Frederick Barbarossa, nephew and successor of Conrad III,
takes part in this Crusade.

The maritime route of the crusaders, after ill success on
land, is noteworthy, and forecasts future events.

1147-9   While the German king is absent on the Crusade, German
expansion is renewed at home, under Henry the Lion of
Saxony, Albert the Bear of Brandenburg, and Conrad of
Wettin, as a crusade against the heathen Slavs (Wends)
of Mecklenburg, Pomerania, &c.   Advances of Teutonic
conquest, colonization, and conversion.

The rebuilding of Lincoln Cathedral finished, in its **1147** Norman form (almost entirely replaced by Gothic, later; see 1123).

Lisbon permanently recovered for Christendom by Affonso **1147** Henriques and his Portuguese, with the aid of crusaders from England, Flanders, &c., on their way to the Holy Land by sea. The city, already one of the greatest towns of Muslim Spain, becomes the capital of the new kingdom of Portugal.

Eleanor of Aquitaine, divorced from Louis VII of France, **1152** marries Henry of Anjou (Henry II of England).

Conrad III chooses as his heir his nephew Frederick of **1152** Swabia : the latter is unanimously elected by the princes of the Empire in Frankfurt-on-Main and crowned at Aacher as Frederick I.

Frederick I, 'Barbarossa' (Red Beard), German king **1152–** and Emperor, one of the chief sovereigns, statesmen, and **1190** warriors of the Middle Ages. The policy of this ' Imperial Hildebrand ' is directed towards a *revival of the fullest imperial authority*, not merely in Germany itself, but in the other possessions of the Empire. Hence his great *struggle against the Papacy and the City Republics of Italy*. Though defeated in S. Europe, he is fairly successful in the German lands, and crushes all movements towards rebellion.

Henry of Anjou lands in England and by the Treaty of **1153** *Wallingford* is recognized as heir to the English Crown.

Commencement of the Baptistery at Pisa (finished **1153** 1278).

Death of King Stephen of England. Henry of Anjou **1154** succeeds as **Henry II,** the head of an **Anglo-Angevin Empire** reaching from the Tyne to the Pyrenees, and including all Western France (in the latter, nominally vassal to the

French king).   In 1169–71, &c., much of the eastern part of Ireland is added to this Empire, which is shattered in 1204 (by the loss of Normandy, &c.).   Henry's work as an administrator makes him one of the leading figures in English history.

1154   The 'Campanile', or bell-tower of St. Mark's, Venice, finished [begun 1148.]

PERIOD XIX

FROM THE MIDDLE OF THE TWELFTH CENTURY TO THE DEFEAT OF THE EMPIRE IN ITALY AND THE MUHAMMADAN RECONQUEST OF JERUSALEM, 1154–87

GENERAL POINTS

1. Vigorous struggle of the **German** kingdom (finally ending in **failure**) to establish real supremacy **in Italy.**

2. The imperial power, defeated in Italy, maintains itself in Germany.

3. Increase in the power and **prosperity of the City Republics of Italy.**

4. Increased strength and security of the Papacy.

5. The **Angevin Empire** at its height.

6. **Muhammadan Revival** in the Levant destroys the Crusading states, except certain fragments.

7. **Progress in Civilization** (literature, art, science, philosophy, &c. Earliest European notice of the magnet in navigation).

1154–5   First expedition of Frederick Barbarossa to Italy, to *restore the full imperial power beyond the Alps*. Frederick crowned King of Italy at Pavia and Emperor at Rome by Adrian IV (Nicholas Breakspear, the only English Pope), who had begged for imperial aid against Roman Republican and heretical movements.

Arnold of Brescia, captured by the imperial forces, handed over to the Church, condemned, and burnt as a heretic.

1156   Austria separated from Bavaria and *created a Duchy*.

1157   Frederick holds an Imperial Diet at Würzburg : embassies from the Eastern Empire, England, Denmark, Hungary.

Submission of the nobles of Burgundy to the Empire at Besançon. Imposing position of the imperial power, to which several Christian states beyond the territorial limits of the Empire now do homage.

1157–63   Frederick attacks Poland, forces it to acknowledgement of the imperial supremacy, and begins the detachment of Silesia from Poland and its attachment to Germany [German colonization here after 1163].

1158   The *Royal Crown and title conferred by Frederick on* the Duke of *Bohemia*.

1158–62   Second expedition of Frederick to Italy. Milan and the other Lombard cities submit.

1158   Diet on the Roncaglian Fields (Piacenza) : the imperial rights over the cities defined.

1160–2   Milan revolts afresh, and is besieged.

1162   On its surrender, after two years' siege, Frederick orders the neighbouring towns to undertake the destruction of its walls and buildings. His order, in great part, obeyed (1162).

1159–62   Meantime, schism in the Papacy. Alexander III (enemy of Frederick Barbarossa, friend and supporter of Thomas Becket) elected by the majority of the Cardinals ; Victor IV

by the imperialist minority.   Alexander defies the imperial
claims in Rome, and excommunicates Frederick, but is
forced to fly from Italy to France (1162).

Travels of the Spanish Jew Benjamin of Tudela in Italy,   c. 1159-
the Byzantine Empire, the lands of the Eastern Caliphate,   1173
&c.   Importance of his record.

Abbey of Crowland in the English Fens completed.   c. 1160
' Leaning Tower ' (Campanile of the Cathedral), Pisa,
finished.

Death of Peter Lombard, the ' Master of the Sentences ',   1160
Bishop of Paris (born *circa* 1100 at Novara, in NW. Italy).
His collection of *Sentences*, or opinions of the Christian
Fathers, became a leading text-book all over Roman
Christendom, and gave rise to many commentaries.   It
is among the most popular and influential works of the
' Schoolmen '.

Erection of the Church of the Templars at Thomar, in   c. 1162
Central Portugal, one of the finest examples of the ' round
Sepulchre church ' in Christendom.

After Frederick's departure, the anti-imperial party in   1163-6
Italy revives.   Pope Alexander returns to Rome.

In England, **Constitutions of Clarendon** [a determined   1164
effort to check the Ecclesiastical power—e.g. beneficed
clergy not to leave the realm without the king's permission ; tenants-in-chief of the Crown not to be excommunicated without the king's knowledge ; villeins not to be
ordained without their lords' consent ; criminous clerks
to be brought under the jurisdiction of the king's court,
and, if found guilty, not to be protected by the Church].

Assize of Clarendon revises the provincial administra-   1166
tion of justice in England.   Jury of Presentment ordered
in criminal cases.   General visitation of England by Itinerant
Justices.

1164–7   **Formation of the** (anti-imperial) **Lombard League** (Cremona, Brescia, Mantua, Verona, Padua, &c.).

1166–8   Frederick's Fourth Italian Expedition. The Emperor escorts his anti-Pope Paschal III (successor of Victor IV) to Rome ; Alexander taking refuge, like Gregory VII, with the Normans of S. Italy.

1168   Frederick's unsuccessful siege of Rome. His army destroyed by pestilence. The Emperor escapes over the Alps, almost without attendants. Rebuilding of Milan by the Lombard League.

1168   Foundation of Alessandria (so named after Pope Alexander III, the friend and ally of the League).

1169   **Overthrow of the Supremacy of Kiev in Russia** (since *c.* 880 Kiev has been the head of the Russian principalities, race, and religion). After this the supremacy fluctuates between various principalities [Vladimir, Suzdal, &c.], and finally passes to Moscow in the fourteenth century.

c. 1170   Poem of *The Cid* (Spanish Romantic literature).

c. 1170   Earliest (?) notices of the Waldenses—' Protestants of the Middle Ages ' [cf. note on the Albigenses, p. 134].

1170   Murder of Thomas Becket in his own Cathedral of Canterbury. Reaction in favour of the Church in its conflict with the secular power; e. g. with Henry II in England and the Angevin lands, Frederick Barbarossa in Germany, Italy, Burgundy, &c.

1174–8   Frederick's Fifth Italian Expedition. Fruitless siege of Alessandria by the imperialists. Disaffection among the German forces. Henry the Lion refuses to follow the Emperor, who is now opposed by the whole strength of the Lombard League and the Papacy, aided by the Eastern Empire [Manuel Komnenos, see p. 118].

1176   *Battle of Legnano* (sixteen miles north-west of Milan). Decisive defeat of the imperialists.

End of the Italian war. *Frederick admits his defeat,* accepts in principle the main demands of the Italian cities and the Pope, and sets himself to minimize his misfortunes, and especially to secure his position at home in Germany [see 1183].

Assize of Northampton.   Instructions to Itinerant **1176** Justices.

Meeting and 'reconciliation' of Pope and Emperor at **1177** Venice.

Frederick is crowned King of Burgundy at Arles, and **1178** returns to Germany [note the connexion still maintained at the close of the twelfth century between the Burgundian kingdom, including Lyons and all the SE. of Modern France, and the Holy Roman Empire of the German nation].

Frederick Barbarossa triumphant over rebellious move- **1180–1** *ments in Germany.* Submission of Henry the Lion of Saxony, the chief leader of these movements ; banished for three years, he goes to the court of Henry II of England, his father-in-law.   Division of the Duchy of Saxony, large parts of it becoming 'immediate' possessions of the Empire (e.g. Holstein, Schwerin, Oldenburg, Lübeck, &c.) ; other portions fall to Bernhard of Askania, son of Albert the Bear ; to the See of Cologne ; and to Bavaria (House of Wittelsbach).   Frederick thus pursues his imperial and national policy—to weaken the great duchies by dividing them.

Methods of Insurance begin to be popular in some parts **c. 1180–** of Europe, especially in the Commercial Republics of **1190,** Italy. **&c.**

Earliest clear [European] references to the **use of the** **c. 1180–** **magnetic needle in navigation,** in the works of Alexander **1186** Neckam of St. Albans and Paris.   From these references it is clear that the practical use of the compass had been established for some time among certain European seamen. Probably this first took place in Italy, in one of the commercial republics (Amalfi, Genoa, Pisa, or Venice ?).

1183   Final **Peace of Constance** between the Empire and the Lombard cities. By this the Italian cities are ' maintained in all the regalian rights, whether within their walls or in their district, which they could claim by usage . . . especially . . . those of levying war, erecting fortifications, administering civil and criminal justice . . . and nominating their consuls or other magistrates, who were to receive investiture of office from an imperial legate. The Emperor was authorized to appoint in every city a judge of appeal in civil causes. The Lombard League was confirmed, and the cities were . . . to renew it at . . . discretion, but . . . to take every ten years an oath of fidelity to the Emperor ' [see 1176].

1184–6   Frederick Barbarossa, on his sixth and last Italian visit (wholly peaceful), marries his son Henry (the future Emperor Henry VI) to Constance, daughter of the Norman king Roger II, heiress of the Norman kingdom in S. Italy and Sicily. ' Legnano neutralized.'

c. 1185   *Saladin* (Salah-ud-Din Yusuf), Sultan of Egypt from 1173, master of Muhammadan Syria by 1183 (conquest of Aleppo), becomes *supreme in the Muslim world of the Levant*, and prepares his decisive attack upon the Crusading states.

1185   The Temple Church in London (the round church) completed, and consecrated by the Patriarch of Jerusalem, then on a visit to W. Europe to procure aid against Saladin.

1187   **Saladin** destroys the crusading army near the Sea of Galilee (battle of the Horns of Hattin, July 4), **takes Jerusalem** (October 2), and **conquers almost all Christian Syria.**

PERIOD XX

FROM THE FALL OF THE LATIN KINGDOM OF JERUSALEM TO THE LATERAN COUNCIL OF 1215, AND THE GRANTING OF THE GREAT CHARTER IN ENGLAND, 1187–1215

GENERAL POINTS

1. The power of the (**Hildebrandine**) **Papacy at its height.**

2. The **Third Crusade,** the last real exertion of the full strength of Western Christendom in the Syrian Holy War. Partial success ; predominant failure.

3. A fresh ' Latin expansion ' eastwards marked by the **Fourth Crusade,** and the foundation of a ' **Latin Empire** ' **of Constantinople,** conclusive evidence of the perversion of the crusading spirit and movement.

4. *Fatal weakening of the Eastern Empire,* so long the chief bulwark of Europe and Christendom in the Levant.

5. **Rise of Venice** to a dominant commercial and naval position in the Levant (and more or less over the whole Mediterranean), another consequence of the Fourth Crusade.

6. Victorious **struggle of the Latin Church with heresy in** S. France, &c. **Beginnings of the Inquisition and of the Friars.**

7. Destruction, in large measure, of the Anglo-Angevin Empire in France.

8. First real appearance of the **great French monarchy.**

9. **Promise of a new English** (Anglo-Norman) **Nationality and of English liberties.**

10. Decisive success of the Spanish Crusade. **Break-up of Muslim power in Andalusia.**

11. **Developments in civilization** (literature, art, science, philosophy, &c. Buildings ; University progress).

1187-9   Immense excitement in Christendom resulting from the fall of the kingdom of Jerusalem. Preaching of a new Crusade (the third, 1189-92), in which the Emperor Frederick Barbarossa, Richard I of England, and Philip II (called afterwards ' Augustus ') of France, take part.

1188   *Saladin Tithe* in England, the *first English taxation of Personality* or movable property (somewhat anticipated in *Assize of Arms*, 1181).

1189-92   The **Third Crusade** : (*a*) the Emperor Frederick, starting from Ratisbon, goes overland to Asia Minor, captures Kuniyah (Iconium), and is drowned in Cilicia (1190). Many of the German crusaders return. The rest go on to Palestine by way of Antioch and Tyre, help these cities against the Saracens, and take part in the siege of Acre.

(*b*) Richard Cœur de Lion and Philip Augustus go by sea, joining forces at Marseilles (1190), and making six months' stay in Sicily (September 1190—March 1191). On the way to Acre, Richard overruns Cyprus (May 1191). *Acre*, besieged by crusading forces since August 28, 1189, *surrenders* July 12, 1191, in spite of the desperate attempts of Saladin to relieve it.

Relations between French and English kings and crusaders grow worse. Philip returns home. Richard, unable to retake Jerusalem, in spite of wonders of bravery and daring, makes terms with Saladin (September 1192). *Truce for three years*, three months, three days, three hours ; *recognition of coastal strip from Acre to Ascalon as crusading territory.* Freedom of pilgrimage to holy places. Richard returns by the Adriatic and Vienna, where he is seized (December 1192), handed over to the Emperor, and held prisoner.

The Austrian banner, it is said, perhaps with truth, had been trodden in the filth at Acre by Richard's order ; but his imprisonment by the Emperor is no doubt mainly due to Richard's alliance with the Guelfic party in Germany, and to the imperial ambitions (extension of suzerainty over England, &c.).

Henry, son of Frederick Barbarossa, left behind in Ger- **1190** many as regent, succeeds as the Emperor Henry VI— a ruler of the highest gifts, whose early death (1197) changes the history of Europe.

First legal recognition of the *Communa or Corporation* **1191** *of London* (the twelfth century is an **age of town growth** in many parts of Europe—e. g. England, Germany, Flanders, Italy, France).

Henry VI makes his first expedition to Italy, is crowned **1191** emperor in Rome, but fails to take Naples.

Fresh struggles of the imperial power in Germany with **1192–4** Henry the Lion and the Guelfs, ended by a settlement which included (*a*) the release of Richard Cœur-de-Lion, after thirteen months' imprisonment, mainly in the Rhineland (Trifels and Worms), on payment of a large ransom, the rendering of homage, and the promise of tribute to the Empire ; (*b*) a marriage alliance between the imperial house and that of Henry the Lion.

Henry VI makes another expedition to Italy, conquers **1194** the Two Sicilies, and re-establishes imperial authority, for the moment, over much of Central Italy.

Richard Cœur-de-Lion returns to England, suppresses **1194** rebellion, and opens war with Philip of France.

Great part of Chartres Cathedral, destroyed by fire, is **1194,** rebuilt. [The work goes on through the first half of the **&c.** thirteenth century.]

Battle of Alarcos [or Alarcon] in Central Spain (New **1195** Castile). Apparently overwhelming, but really indecisive, victory of the Muhammadans, under the Almohade Caliph, Yakub Al Mansur.

1196   Henry VI puts forward a plan for making the German kingdom an hereditary monarchy, and all its fiefs hereditary. Successful opposition of the German nobles.

1196   Death of Walter Map (Mapes), Archdeacon of Oxford, Anglo-Norman satirist (*Golias*).

1197   Last expedition of Henry VI to Italy. His death (at age of thirty-two) interrupts gigantic schemes for extension of German imperial power.

1197   Richard builds 'Château Gaillard' (' Saucy Castle '), one of the most important and typical of mediaeval castles —near the frontier of Normandy, to command the Seine and guard against French attack.

1198– **Pontificate of Innocent III**—the most powerful and
1216 successful of all the Roman pontiffs in history. **The influence of the Latin Church**, in general, throughout Europe is now **at its zenith,** and remains so throughout the thirteenth century.

1198   Death of ' Averroes ' (Ibn Rashid), most celebrated and important of Arabic philosophers, physicians, and men of science in Spain. Leading representative of the Muslim culture of the West, especially at Cordova. His Aristotelian translations and commentaries (' Averroes, who the great comment made ' in Dante, *Inferno*, iv).

1198– Civil war in Germany. On death of Henry VI, Philip
1208 of Swabia, youngest son of Barbarossa, is elected by the Hohenstaufen party ; Otto IV of Brunswick, son of Henry the Lion, by the Guelf party supported by the Church. The latter is saved from complete defeat by the murder of Philip (1208). Otto generally recognized.

1199   Death of Richard Cœur-de-Lion. Accession of John to the Anglo-Angevin Empire. Rival claims of his nephew Arthur, son of Geoffrey Plantagenet, brother of Henry II of England, who takes refuge at the French Court. Truce between Philip Augustus and John.

Castle of Vincennes, near Paris, begun *c.* 1164 by **c. 1200**
Louis VII, is completed, in its earlier form, by Philip
Augustus. No castle in Europe is more typical of the
'feudal age' than the keep of Vincennes, 170 feet high,
of extraordinary massiveness and strength. It was a
favourite residence of French kings (e. g. Philip Augustus,
Louis X, Charles IV, V, VI, and IX). The four last
named, Henry V of England, and Cardinal Mazarin are
among those who died here. From Louis XI it is one of
the chief state prisons. It was also the birth-place of
Charles V of France.

Introduction of windmills into Europe from the Muham- **Before**
madan East, one of the 'civilizing details' of the Crusades. **1200**

Charter of Philip Augustus to the Schools of Paris.   **1200**

Completion of the main part of the present (Romanesque) **c. 1200**
Cathedral of Worms. Some parts of this building go back
to the eighth century.

Great age of Icelandic literature, at this time, and during **c. 1200**
all the later twelfth and earlier thirteenth centuries. Sagas
(*Heimskringla*, or Sagas of the Norse kings, *Burnt Njal*,
Eyrbyggia, Grettir the Strong, &c.).

Campo Santo at Pisa formed, for burial of leading **c. 1200**
citizens ; earth brought from Jerusalem after Third Crusade.

Great age of Troubadour poetry, especially in S. of France **c. 1100–**
(Toulouse, Provence, &c.), now and during most of twelfth **1200**
century. Bertrand de Born, Viscount of Hautefort, 1145–
1210, is a leading representative of this literature, mainly
concerned with love and war. These Icelandic sagas and
Troubadour songs and poems, carried on by the Trouvères
in N. France, and by the Minnesingers in Germany, are
really the **first important chapters of modern European
literature.** The Troubadours to some extent aid the free-
thinking and anti-Church tendencies of the later twelfth
century.

1202   Philip of France summons John to appear before him as suzerain and explain his oppression of his subjects, especially the barons of Poitou. John refuses to appear, and war begins again.

1202-2   **Fourth Crusade,** organized by Innocent III ; led by Baldwin, Count of Flanders, by Boniface, Marquis of Montferrat, by other northern barons, and later by Henry (Enrico) Dandolo, Doge of Venice. The original purpose was attack upon Egypt and deliverance of Holy Land thereby. But Venice, which furnishes fleet and transports for the northern crusaders, and joins in the Crusade, turns the expedition away from crusading purposes, and makes it the instrument of her aggrandizement. Zara in Dalmatia, a revolted vassal-city of Venice, is taken. Then the crusaders proceed to Constantinople, and restore the exiled Emperor Isaac Angelos, who is to act as their ally and agent (1203). A popular rising breaks out in the city, and Angelos is murdered. A nationalist emperor is set up. Constantinople is besieged and taken by the crusaders, with terrible destruction of historic buildings and works of art (1204). Widespread conflagration.

The conquerors set up a **Latin, or Frankish, Empire** (which lasts till 1261) on the ruins of the East Roman or Byzantine. Baldwin of Flanders first Latin emperor.

The Venetians secure a large share of the spoil—a 'quarter' in Constantinople ; a dominant position in the trade of the Byzantine world, especially in the Aegaean Sea and Black Sea ; the island of Euboea or Negropont ; the Ionian Islands—Corfu, &c. ; the coast of Albania ; a great part of the Peloponnesos or Morea ; Crete, &c.

Frankish principalities are set up in Thrace and Greece, vassals of the new Latin Empire of the East (' Dukes ' of Athens, Thebes, Achaia, &c.). All Europe is lost to the Byzantine for a time. The Byzantine cause is main-

tained in Asia by (a) the ' Greek Empire of Nicaea ' (Nikaia);
(b) the ' Empire of Trebizond '.

The Fourth Crusade marks the **end of the Eastern Empire
as a great Christian state.** Though restored at Constantinople in 1261, and lasting till 1453, it is hopelessly decrepit.
The crusaders of 1204 prepare for the Turks of the fourteenth and fifteenth centuries.

Arthur of Brittany, falling into the power of King John **1203**
of England, disappears. He is universally believed to
have been murdered. Philip of France, as suzerain of the
Angevins on the Continent, is expected to avenge Arthur's
death. Philip invades Normandy.

Philip overruns all Normandy, which is now quite dis- **1204**
loyal to the Anglo-Angevin connexion, and leans to France.
Along with Normandy go Maine, Anjou, Poitou, and
Touraine (and part of Aquitaine). The **Angevin Empire** is
thus **shattered.** Of its vast continental dominions only
part of Aquitaine remains to it. Thus also, territorially,
the **great French Monarchy** is now **founded by Philip
Augustus.**

Death of the ' Hebrew Abelard ', Moses ' Maimonides ', **1204**
great Jewish philosopher and theologian, at Cairo (born
1135, at Cordova).

Chingiz (' Jenghiz ', ' Ghenghiz ') **Khan** recognized as **1206**
supreme chief of the **Mongol** tribes. He begins the conquest
of the outside world, and rapidly creates the largest Asiatic
Empire ever known, and one of the most important in
history.

Stephen Langton, the future leader of the movement **1206–9**
for English liberty (Magna Carta), is chosen as Archbishop
of Canterbury by Innocent III (1206), and duly elected,
but refused admission to England by the king. Innocent
lays England under Interdict (1208–13), and excommunicates John, who seizes Church property (1209).

1208   Murder of Philip of Swabia. Momentary triumph of Otto IV and the Guelf party in Germany.

1209   **Albigensian crusade** (1209–29) begun to check the spread of anti-Church tendencies and sects (Albigenses, Waldenses, Poor Men of Lyons, Cathari, &c.) in S. Europe, especially in S. France, Provence, Toulouse, &c. Albi, NE. of Toulouse, was a head centre of the twelfth-century 'Protestants', among whom two elements must be recognized, (*a*) 'evangelical', (*b*) 'free-thinking'.

1210   St. Francis of Assisi with some difficulty gains the Papal sanction for his (Franciscan) Order of Mendicant Friars.

1211   John still defying the Papacy, Innocent III threatens to depose him, calling on Philip Augustus of France to execute the sentence. Welsh attack on English.

1212   Decisive battle of **Las Navas de Tolosa** in the Sierra Morena in Spain.

Spanish Islam has been repeatedly saved from complete ruin by Muhammadan aid from Africa ('Almoravides' in eleventh century ; 'Almohades' in twelfth ; see 1086, 1160, 1195) ; once more she is hard pressed by the Christian States at the opening of the thirteenth century, and again calls in African allies, but now without success. The Muslims are utterly defeated, and the Christian conquest of Southern Spain begins.

The Muhammadans had already lost nearly all the Castilian plateau, the heart of the peninsula, and the west coast down to Lisbon, and still farther south, but on the east they were still masters almost to the Ebro.

1212   Otto IV having fallen out with Pope Innocent III, the latter, in alliance with the Ghibelline party, puts forward his ward, the young Hohenstaufen Frederick II, son of the Emperor Henry VI, as anti-emperor.

1212   Foundation of the Cathedral of Rheims (present build-

ing). The west façade is 'perhaps the most beautiful piece
of building produced in the Middle Ages '.

Fearing deposition, and planning a great campaign in **1213**
France for the recovery of the Angevin dominions, John
of England yields to Innocent, receives and admits Langton
as Archbishop of Canterbury, and becomes the Pope's
vassal, resigning his kingdom to the Papacy, and receiv-
ing it again as a tributary state, with a yearly payment
of 1,000 marks.

Suggested germ of the English Parliament in the repre- **1213**
sentative assemblies of 1213 (certain towns summoned to
send deputies, in August, to St. Albans [?]; the shires, in
November, to Oxford [?].

John organizes a coalition against France by alliance **1213–14**
with the Emperor Otto IV and the Count of Flanders.
The English barons at first refuse to follow John to France,
but follow him to La Rochelle in 1214.

But the main army of the coalition, under Otto IV, the
Earl of Salisbury, and the Count of Flanders, is utterly
defeated by Philip Augustus at **Bouvines** near Lille in
Flanders, in a battle which secures all the French gains
of 1204, and asserts French military eminence in Europe
(July 27, 1214).   Break-up of the coalition.   ' Modern
France springs from Bouvines.'

Birth of Roger Bacon [see 1294].   **1214**

Otto IV, returning to Germany, practically abandons **1215**
the field to Frederick II, who is generally recognized as
German King and Emperor (and King of the Two Sicilies),
and crowned at Aachen.

John, returning to England, is confronted by the uprising **1215**
of English liberty, championed by the Church and the
baronage (' the Army of God and Holy Church '), and is
forced to sign **Magna Carta**, ' the Great Charter ', at
Runnymede on the Thames near Windsor (June 15, 1215).

Innocent disallows the Great Charter, excommunicates John's opponents, suspends Langton. The English barons offer the crown to Louis, son of Philip Augustus.

1215   **Lateran Council** at Rome under Innocent III. The chief measures : (*a*) the doctrine of **Transubstantiation** (change of substance or essence), in the Eucharist, decreed (application of the Aristotelian philosophy of *substance* and *accidents* to theological dogma). (*b*) **Compulsory auricular confession** laid down—at least once a year every Catholic layman is to confess to a priest. (*c*) **Abolition of the** trial by **ordeal**. (*d*) Full **sanction of Franciscan and Dominican Orders** of Mendicant Friars.

These new religious orders, instead of retiring from the world, aimed at converting it, and became the greatest popular force and the ablest intellectual support of the Latin Church and its system.

Francis of Assisi was born 1182 ; died 1226 ; and was canonized 1228.

> A fit
> Companion over the high seas, to keep
> The bark of Peter to its proper bearings.
> [Dante.]

Dominic of Calahorra in Spain was born about 1170 ; died 1221 ; and was canonized 1233. The latter,

> That athlete consecrate,
> Kind to his own and cruel to his foes,   [Dante.]

took a great part in suppressing, by his preaching, &c., the Albigensian revolt against the Church : also probably some part in the first organization and administration of the **Inquisition,** founded by Innocent III primarily to stamp out the Albigensian and allied movements.

c. 1215   Chingiz Khan and the Mongols conquer great part of N. China and take Peking.

PERIOD XXI

FROM THE LATERAN COUNCIL AND THE GREAT CHARTER TO THE FINAL DEFEAT OF THE EMPIRE IN ITS STRUGGLE WITH THE PAPACY, 1215-50

GENERAL POINTS

1. **Final struggle of Papacy and Empire. Defeat of the Empire. Fatal weakening of the German kingdom.**

2. **Victory of the Church in its struggle with heresy.** Immense power and prosperity of the Church all through this, the greatest mediaeval, century.

3. Last age of the Palestine Crusades. **Decay of crusading spirit** (for Syria).

4. **Progress of the French kingdom.** Its gains from the Albigensian crusade.

5. **Progress of the Christian kingdoms in Spain.** Spanish Islam confined to Granada. Christian reconquest of Cordova and Seville.

6. **German racial expansion** eastwards (the *Drang nach Osten*). Conquest of Old Prussia.

7. **Progress of civilization.** Gothic architecture at its height. Great age of mediaeval universities, of scholasticism, &c.

8. **Growth of the Mongol Empire,** which now becomes the chief world-power. Mongol conquest of Central Asia, of North China, of Russia. Temporary overrunning of Poland, Hungary, &c. **Commencement of** diplomatic **intercourse between Western Christendom and the Mongols** (from 1245).

c. 1215   About the beginning of the thirteenth century hot-air baths (imitated from Muhammadan) become customary in many European Christian towns.

1216   A French army lands in England under the Dauphin Louis, ' to deliver the nation from John's tyranny '.

1216   Death of Innocent III (July).   Honorius III succeeds.

1216   Death of King John of England (October), at war with the baronage, the Church, and most of the people.   John's little son Henry (III of England) succeeds ;   William Marshall, Earl of Pembroke, regent.   England rallies to the new sovereign.   Reissue of Magna Carta.

1217   The French and their supporters in England defeated by land and sea (Lincoln, May ; Dover, August).   Henry III is generally recognized, and Louis leaves.

1219   Great **Mongol attack on Central Asia and the West** begins :   (a) On Muhammadan Central Asia.   Between 1219 and 1225 Chingiz Khan conquers Bukhara, Samarkand, Khiva, Farghana, N. Afghanistan, N. and E. Persia, much of Caucasia, &c.   (b) From Caucasia a Mongol army attacks the Russians about 1223.   Great Mongol victory, near the Sea of Azov, on the river Kalka (May 31).   But, for the moment, the attack is not pressed ; the Mongols retire beyond the Caucasus, to return in 1236.   The death of Chingiz (1227), and the Chinese conquests of the next few years, call their attention away from Europe.

1220   Coronation of Frederick II as emperor at Rome.   He renews his vow of crusade (taken 1215).

1220   Commencement of (the present) Salisbury Cathedral [see 1260, 1350].

1220   Henry III of England begins the rebuilding of Westminster Abbey, destroying the Norman Church of Edward the Confessor.

Cathedral of Amiens designed and commenced [see **1220,** 1288]. **&c.**

Birth of Bonaventura, schoolman and mystic [see 1274]. **1221**

Beginnings of the University of Padua. **1222**

Death of Philip Augustus of France [see 1204, 1214]. **1223**
Death of Gerald de Barri, ' Giraldus Cambrensis '—
Welsh-Norman churchman, statesman, and historian (*Itine-
rarium Cambriae*).

Frederick II, as King of the Two Sicilies, founds the **1224**
University of Naples.

Practically all Aristotle is now accessible to W. Christen- **c. 1225**
dom in Latin translations.

The Order of Teutonic Knights—' the German order ', **1226**
founded 1190, during the Third Crusade and the siege of
Acre, as a brotherhood for the care of the sick and wounded,
made an order of religious knighthood 1198—is **commissioned** by Frederick II, at the suggestion of the Grand-
Master Hermann of Salza, and at the invitation of the
Polish Duke Conrad of Mazovia, **to conquer** and ' convert '
the heathen Prussians. This difficult task is accomplished
between 1230 and 1283 by long and bloody wars. In 1237
the Teutonic order unites with the ' Brethren of the Sword ',
who had conquered Livonia and founded Riga in 1201, &c.

[Or perhaps 1224 or 1225] Birth of Thomas of Aquino **c. 1227**
(' Aquinas '), chief of the Schoolmen [see 1274].

Death of Chingiz Khan, succeeded by Okkodai, ' the **1227**
conqueror of Russia, Poland, and Hungary '.
Quarrel between the Papacy and the Emperor Frederick II (accused of postponing and evading the execution
of his vow of crusade). Frederick excommunicated.

Accession of Louis IX (' St. Louis ') of France, under **1228**
whom the French kingdom makes further progress, and
becomes perhaps the most powerful of Christian states.

1228-9   *Fifth Crusade,* led by Frederick II.   Partial success. Jerusalem temporarily recovered, together with Nazareth and Sidon, by treaty with the Sultan of Egypt.   Frederick crowns himself in the Holy City as king of the restored kingdom of Jerusalem.   But all these hopes are soon disappointed.   Jerusalem is finally lost 1244.

1229   End of the **Albigensian crusade,** mainly to the **profit of the French kingdom,** which now annexes the County of Toulouse, and becomes nearly as powerful in the south (towards the Mediterranean) as Philip Augustus had made her in the north (towards the Channel and the Ocean).

1229   Christian conquest of the Balearics, by James 'the Conqueror' of Aragon.

1230   Peace between the Empire and the Papacy at San Germano.

c. 1230   Appearance of the German legal code known as the *Sachsenspiegel* (' Saxon-Mirror ') ;   followed, about 1276, by the *Schwabenspiegel* (' Swabian-Mirror ').

1230   **Final union of Leon and Castile** under Ferdinand III (' St. Ferdinand '), the conqueror of Andalusia.

c. 1231, &c.   The University of Cambridge clearly appears as an organized body, under a chancellor.   **Great age of university progress** at this time (Oxford ; Naples ; Padua ; Salamanca ; College of the Sorbonne ; Lisbon or Coimbra, &c.). See 1200, 1222, 1224, 1241, 1243, 1290.

1231   Weakening of the central power in Germany through the concessions of Frederick II to lay and spiritual lords in the Reichstag at Worms (largely caused by the struggle of the Empire with the Church and the Lombard cities).

1232   Clock and orrery sent to Frederick II by the Sultan of Egypt.

Fall of Hubert de Burgh, and *practical end of the Grand* **1232**
Justiciary in England. The *Chancellor gradually succeeds
the Justiciar* as the practical First Minister of the State.

Personal government of Henry III. Growth of the
movement for the strengthening of English liberties,
especially through the creation of a central representative
assembly, or Parliament.

Birth of Raymond Lull [see 1315].   **1234**

Imperial Reichstag at Mainz. *First known publication* **1235**
of a Law of the Empire in German.

Death of Walther von der Vogelweide, chief of the early **1235**
German poets (Minnesingers), stanch defender of the
imperial claims, and friend of the poor and oppressed
classes.

Great Mongol-Tartar attack on Europe, led by Batu, **1236-43**
grandson of Chingiz Khan, and the brilliant strategist
Subudai. **Conquest,** and temporary ruin, **of all the Russian
states,** except Old Novgorod (near the Baltic), which
submits to tribute. Defeat of the Poles and Hungarians.
Terrible ravaging of Hungary. **Permanent occupation of
much of the present Russia-in-Europe** (including the steppe
lands of the south, and the middle and lower Volga) by the
Mongols, who gradually fix their western capital at Sarai,
a little north of Astrakhan. This Western Mongol sub-
kingdom becomes known as *Kipchak* or *the Golden Horde* ;
later it divides into the khanates of Astrakhan, Kazan,
and Krim.

Castilian conquest of Cordova, by St. Ferdinand [see **1236**
1248].

Victory of Frederick II over the Lombard cities at **1237**
Cortenuova. The Papacy accuses him of heresy.

Union of the Teutonic Knights with the Knights of the
Sword in one Teutonic Order.

c. 1237–1244   Earliest certain notices of Berlin in history [as one of two little fishing villages and townships, Berlin and Cöln]. Not till 1495 does Berlin become the capital of Brandenburg and the official residence of the Elector.

1238   Aragonese conquest of Valencia (by James I 'the Conqueror ').

1239   Frederick II excommunicated afresh by Pope Gregory IX.

1240   Choir of old St. Paul's, London, rebuilt in Gothic style, and new tower commenced.

1240   The Cathedral of Chartres completed (main part). The Baptistery of Pisa Cathedral completed.

1240–1   The Mongols ravage Silesia, but are checked by a German army at Wahlstatt, near Liegnitz. They retire SE. and invade Hungary.

c. 1240–1250   Completion of the main part of the Cathedral of Chartres.

1241   Alliance between the cities of Lübeck and Hamburg, which grows into the Hanseatic League.

1241   Beginnings of the University of Siena (charter from the Emperor Charles IV, 1357).

1243   The University of Salamanca founded by Ferdinand III.

1244   Pope Innocent IV (1243–4) flies before Frederick II out of Italy to Lyons.

1245   Death of Alexander of Hales, ' the Irrefragable Doctor ', one of the leading English Schoolmen (? teacher of Bonaventura). His chief works were written in Paris.

1245   Council of Lyons. Excommunication of Frederick II renewed, and his deposition now declared. The German princes summoned to make a new election.

1245   John de Plano Carpini sent as Papal Envoy to the Mongols, thus **opening intercourse between Western Christendom and the Tartars.** Carpini traverses Russia

and Central Asia, and penetrates to the Great Khan's camp
in Mongolia, south of Lake Baikal.

Immense **extension of the boundaries of European knowledge.** Discovery of inner Asia, almost to China. Carpini's
contact with Chinese, in Mongolia.

The twelfth-century translation of Euclid by Adelard **1246**
of Bath is edited by Campanus of Novara. From this
came the first printed edition (of 1482).

Anti-kings in Germany—Heinrich Raspe, Landgrave of **1246–56**
Thuringia, 1246–7 ; William of Holland, 1247–56—set up
(mainly by the Church) against Frederick II and his
successor.

Seville taken by St. Ferdinand of Castile [see 1236].   **1248**

Sixth Crusade, undertaken by St. Louis (Louis IX) of **1248–56**
France, who sails from Aigues-Mortes. Forming his base
in Cyprus, he thence attacks the Muslim power in Egypt.
Here he takes Damietta, but on the way to Cairo is defeated
and taken prisoner with all his army (April 1250). Liberated
on terms of surrendering Damietta and paying a ransom,
Louis goes to Palestine, where he spends almost four years,
fortifying Acre, Sidon, and other crusading strongholds
on the coast. (His work at Sidon is still standing.)

The still existing fortifications of Aigues-Mortes, one of the **1248,&c.**
most interesting remains of the Middle Ages, commenced
by St. Louis (?) ; mostly built under Philip III, 1270–85.

Beginning of (the present Gothic) Choir of Cologne **1248**
Cathedral.

Germ of University College, Oxford, in endowments by **1249**
William of Durham.

Completion of Aragonese and Portuguese conquests from **1250**
the Muhammadans in Spain. These two states now attain
their final extent in the Peninsula. Castile still lacks the
SE. extremity, where the last stand of Islam is made in the

kingdom of Granada (not absorbed till 1492, by Ferdinand and Isabella, of the United Spanish monarchy).

1250   **Death of Frederick II in Apulia.** ' **With Frederick fell the Empire.** . . . From the ruin that overwhelmed the greatest of its houses (the Hohenstaufen), it emerged, living indeed . . . but so shattered, crippled, and degraded, that it could never be to Europe and to Germany what it once had been ' [Bryce].

c. 1250, Completion of the main part of Lincoln Cathedral, in
&c. Gothic style.

c. 1250 Berry Pomeroy Castle in Devon (oldest existing parts) ; Carisbrooke Castle in the Isle of Wight (most of the existing building outside the keep).

Causes of the failure and wreck of the Empire and the German kingdom in the thirteenth century :

(1) the imperfect unification, and strong disruptionist tendencies of Germany ; (and arising out of this)

1 *a.* The ruinous concessions to the feudal lords.

Behind all this,

1 *b.* The elective character of the Crown and its want of identification with any particular leading tribe, race, or region, in Germany, is a primary source of weakness.

2. The Italian connexion and the sacrifice of imperial and German interests to this ; (and arising out of this)

2 *a.* The quarrel with the Italian Republics.

3. The quarrel with the Papacy and the Ultramontane party throughout the Empire.

c. 1250 Foundation of Stockholm. It does not, however, become the capital of Sweden till much later (fourteenth century). There is no fixed ' capital ' in this country in earlier centuries.

PERIOD XXII

FROM THE DEATH OF FREDERICK II TO THE END OF THE PALESTINE CRUSADES, 1250-70

GENERAL POINTS

1. Paralysis of the German kingdom and Western Empire (ruined by its struggle with the Papacy). The **Great Interregnum in Germany.** Widespread anarchy.

2. Beginnings of the **Hanseatic League** of commercial cities (in reaction from anarchy).

3. Continued development of **German racial expansion** eastwards (in Baltic coast-lands).

4. End of the Latin Empire of Constantinople. **Restoration of the Eastern Empire** in Byzantine form. Feeble old age of the restored Empire.

5. Depression of Venice and rise of Genoa in the Levant, &c., consequent upon (4). The **great age of Genoa** now begins.

6. **Cessation of the Syrian Crusades,** the last two being directed against Muhammadan Africa.

7. **Progress of the French kingdom** continued.

8. **Development of English liberties.** The English **Parliament** begins to take complete form, as a national representative assembly.

9. Similar development of liberties in Spanish Christian states [Castile, Aragon, &c.].

10. Progress of **Mongol power and conquests** [e.g. in

China, Persia]. Further development of intercourse between Mongols and W. Christendom.

10 *a*. End of the Eastern [Baghdad] Caliphate, destroyed by Mongols.

11. Progress of civilization.   Zenith of Gothic architecture and of scholasticism.   Development of city life. Advances in science, literature, and art.   The **Church** still **at the height of its influence,** dominating European civilization.

Conrad IV, son and successor of Frederick II, wastes **1250-4**
his strength in Italy, captures Naples, dies of fever. All
this time the anti-king, William of Holland, is active in
Germany.

The *Alfonsine Tables* compiled under patronage of **1252**
Alphonso X, ' the Learned ', of Castile and Leon. Advance
in mediaeval astronomy.

Louis IX sends the Franciscan William of Rubrouck **1253-5**
(Rubruquis), a French Fleming, as his envoy to the Mongols.
Rubrouck, like Carpini, goes to the Great Khan's camp
in Mongolia (now at Karakorum).

Both these Friar travellers, *the first discoverers of the
bulk of Asia for Europe*, leave valuable accounts of their
missions, and of the state of the Mongol world at that
time.

Rubrouck declares the inland character of the Caspian,
which is recognized from this time.

Death of Conrad IV of Germany.   **1254**

Death of William of Holland.   **1256**

The Great Interregnum in Germany. Ruin of the unity **1256-73**
and strength of the German kingdom as a whole.

' Every floodgate of anarchy was opened : prelates and
barons extended their domains by war ; robber-knights
infested highways and rivers ; the misery of the weak, the
tyranny of the strong, were such as had not been seen for
centuries. . . . Only in the cities (and the Alps) was shelter
or peace to be found ' [Bryce].

This is the time of the early **growth of the Hansa or
Hanseatic League.** Also of the early importance of the
legal codes of the *Sachsenspiegel* and the *Schwabenspiegel*
(see above), and of the secret tribunals of the *Fem-(Vehm-)-
gerichte*, especially in Westphalia.

(There is no real and complete restoration of the German
nation and kingdom till the nineteenth century, through

the work of Bismarck and others, under William I of Prussia.)

Now, after the Interregnum, there is a notable *increase of the power of the feudal lords*, great and small, and in the importance *of the cities*. Certain outlying districts, e.g. the Swiss mountains, where the old local freedom has always been strong, refuse to submit to the encroachments of lords, and gradually achieve complete independence. 'The German kingdom broke down beneath the weight of the . . . Empire' [Bryce].

1244-58 Growing opposition to the misrule of Henry III in England (led from 1257 by Simon de Montfort, Earl of Leicester), culminates in the Parliament and *Provisions of Oxford* (1258). By the Oxford *Provisions* the Government is practically put 'in commission', under baronial control, being entrusted to temporary or standing committees. The chief of these is the Council of Fifteen, permanent advisers of the Crown, chosen partly by representatives of the king and his party, partly by representatives of the opposition. The monarchy thus becomes strictly 'constitutional' and 'limited', but much of its power is soon restored (from 1265).

1260 Completion of Salisbury Cathedral, except the spire [see 1220, 1350].

1260-70 First journey of the two elder Polos (Nicolò and Maffeo, Venetian merchants) in the Mongol world—to Russia, Central Asia, and China. They reach the court of Kublai Khan at Peking, and begin the European discovery of the Far East.

1261 'Restoration' of the Byzantine Empire by Michael Palaiologos (from Nicaea).

1263 Civil war in England, resulting from Henry's struggles against the Provisions of Oxford.

Balliol College, Oxford, begun by John Balliol, of **1263–8**
Barnard Castle, Durham, and Dervorguilla, parents of
John Balliol, King of Scotland.

Death of Vincent of Beauvais [b. 1190 ?], one of the **c. 1264**
chief encyclopaedists of the Middle Ages, author of vast
collections of material for theology, history, and the study
of nature—the *Speculum Doctrinale*, *Spec. Historiale*, and
Spec. Naturale—summaries of the knowledge of the
thirteenth century.

Louis IX of France annuls the Provisions of Oxford by **1264**
the *Mise of Amiens*. Henry III defeated at Lewes by
Simon de Montfort and the constitutional party.

' **Simon de Montfort's Parliament** ', a ' party assembly ', **1265**
but the first in which the full English national representation was realized, and where town members, county
members, clergy, and baronage met (January 1265). See
1275, 1295.

Fresh outbreak of the Civil War. Prince Edward (after-
wards Edward I) escapes and leads the king's party.
Simon de Montfort defeated and killed in the battle of
Evesham (August 4).

Birth of Duns Scotus, the Schoolman [see 1308].   **? 1265**

The *Dictum de Kenilworth* nominally *restores the power of* **1266**
the monarchy, and annuls the Provisions of Oxford, but
Prince Edward now really directs the government ; royal
misgovernment is ended or at least checked ; and the
Crown itself fosters the growth of Parliament.

Fall of the Hohenstaufen in S. Italy. The ' kingdom **1266–8**
of the Two Sicilies ' granted by the Pope to Charles of
Anjou, brother of St. Louis of France, who conquers it
and kills Manfred, the son, and Conradin, the grandson,
of Frederick II.

'The Norman kings (of S. Italy) were more terrible in
their death than in their life : they had sometimes baffled

the Teutonic Emperor : their heritage destroyed him. . . .
In the last act of the tragedy were joined the enemy who
had now blighted the strength of the Empire (the Papacy),
and the rival destined to insult its weakness and blot out
its name ' (France) [Bryce].

1268   Final loss of Antioch by the Crusaders.

1268   Return of the elder Polos from their first journey to the
East.   They bring back the earliest first-hand European
knowledge of China, and strong encouragement to develop
intercourse with the Tartar world (e. g. an invitation, from
Kublai to the Pope, to send Christian teachers to the
Mongols).

1268   Roger Bacon, at the invitation of Pope Clement IV,
issues his *Opus Maius, Opus Minus,* and *Opus Tertium,*
the chief mediaeval anticipation of modern natural science
and ' inductive philosophy ', ' the *Encyclopaedia* and
Organon of the thirteenth century ' [Whewell].

1270   Seventh and *last of* ' *the Crusades,*' led by Louis IX of
France, joined by Prince Edward of England.
Louis endeavours this time to attack the Muslim power
first in the West, and besieges Tunis, before which he
dies.
Prince Edward goes to Syria, but effects nothing.

Before   The Castle of Angers, as now existing, completed by
1270   Louis IX (' still one of the most imposing ' mediaeval
fortresses ' in existence, although several of its towers
have been razed ', and its vast moat filled up).

Before   Completion of the fortifications of Carcassonne, a double
1270   line of ramparts and towers, one of the best illustrations
in any country of a mediaeval fortified city.
(Aiques Mortes fortifications in the next few years.)

PERIOD XXIII

FROM THE END OF THE SYRIAN CRUSADES TO THE FALL OF THE HILDEBRANDINE PAPACY, 1270–1303

GENERAL POINTS

1. **The last age of the Hildebrandine Papacy** and its **fall.**

2. Appearance of the principle of **nationality as a leading force** in European politics.

3. **Strength of the French kingdom,** now (under Philip the Fair) the most powerful state in Christendom.

4. **Strength of the English kingdom.** Struggle for an empire of the British Isles.

5. **Beginnings of the Swiss Confederation.**

6. Close of the Interregnum in Germany. Partial restoration of national prosperity and political life.

7. Progress of German trade and expansion (Hansa and Teutonic Order).

8. **Disappearance of the last fragments of Crusading dominion in Syria.**

9. Development of the **European expansion.** Complete discovery (for Europe) of China and the whole Mongol Empire, of great part of the Indies, &c. Beginnings of exploration and colonization in the Atlantic. First attempt to find the ocean way round Africa to India.

10. **Developments of Civilization.** Mediaeval Thought and Art (Scholasticism, Architecture, &c.) continue in their most brilliant phases.

Beginnings of the Higher Mediaeval Literature.

c. 1270   About this time the **great 'Mongol trade-routes '**—(*a*) from the Black Sea, (*b*) from the Mediterranean, to NW. Persia ; (*c*) from NW. Persia to the Indian Ocean and the mouth of the Persian Gulf ; (*d*) from NW. Persia to Central Asia ; (*e*) from the Black Sea and the Azov to Central Asia and China—begin to be used by European merchants, missionaries, diplomatists, adventurers, &c. Along these lines the 'overland expansion' of Europe in Asiatic fields is mainly carried on during the Mongol Age (to *c.* 1370).

From West Central Asia to China three main routes are followed : (i) north of the Thian Shan range ; (ii) south of the Thian Shan ; (iii) north of the Kuen Lun range. All these three united at the W. end of the Great Wall of China and followed the line of that rampart to the Hoangho.

c. 1270-   Earlier buildings of the Moorish palace-fortress of the
1273   *Alhambra* (Al Hamra, ' the Red ') completed in Granada [see 1390].   Completion of the main part of Amiens Cathedral.

1271   Pope Gregory X (1271-6), ' the noblest spirit and the truest Christian among the Hildebrandine popes ', commissions the Polos, with others, as envoys of Christendom in a second journey to Asia, the Far East, and the Mongol courts (1271-95).   Young Marco Polo (now 17), son of Nicolò, accompanies his relatives, and becomes the describer of the lands visited by the Polos (in the *Book of Marco Polo*).

Before   Buildings of Henry III of England at Windsor Castle
1272   (the great Round Tower reconstructed by Edward III, the great hall, kitchen, chapel, &c.).

1272   Death of Henry III and accession of Edward I of England (' the English Justinian ').

The Chancellor, from about this time, becomes the chief **c. 1273**
Minister of the English State (and so remains till about
1558 and the accession of Elizabeth).

Close of the Great Interregnum in Germany, by the election **1273**
of Rudolf of Hapsburg (i.e. Habsburg in the Aargau, near
Brugg), a chief lord and landowner in 'Switzerland'
proper, landgrave in Alsace. This election is largely
brought about by the efforts of Pope Gregory X, seconded
by the Burggrave of Nuremberg, Frederick III of Hohenzollern. [Here beg﹐s the connexion with the imperial
throne of that family which at last secured the hereditary
possession of the same.]

The (present) Cathedral of Upsala commenced [see **c. 1273**
1100].

Second Council of Lyons. Nominal (and momentary) **1274**
reunion of the Greek and Latin Churches (by submission
of the former to the Pope). Efforts to organize a fresh
Palestine Crusade.

Complete foundation of Merton College at Oxford, 'in **1274**
the true sense of the word, the oldest surviving college in
England' (1264 at Maldon, Surrey). The library, of the
later fourteenth century, is the oldest library-building in
England.

Death of *Thomas Aquinas* (Thomas ' of Aquino ', in the **1274**
territory of Naples), greatest of the schoolmen, author of
the *Summa Theologiae* [see 1227].

English ' shire-knights ', citizens, and burgesses meet in **1275**
the Easter Parliament of this year, which thus carries on
the tradition of 1265, and to a large extent anticipates
1295 [see 1265, 1295].

The Polos arrive at the court of Kublai Khan, Mongol- **1275**
Chinese Emperor (at Peking).

Genoese attempt (finally unsuccessful) to conquer and **c. 1275** colonize in the Northern Canaries. This forms a new starting-point for modern colonial history, as well as for modern European knowledge of the Atlantic.

c. 1276   Vienna becomes a possession of the Hapsburgs.

1276   Death of Pope Gregory X, under whom the 'Hildebrandine Papacy' achieves its last conspicuous successes.

1277   The English conquest of Wales almost completed (the Snowdon region and Anglesea alone left).

1278   Death of Nicolò Pisano, architect and sculptor.

1278   Rudolf of Hapsburg defeats Ottokar II of Bohemia and crushes his attempt to build up a great Bohemian state. By this victory—finally secured by the battle of the Marchfeld, close to Vienna—Rudolf **founds the great Austrian state** instead (nucleus of this in Duchy of Austria, Styria, Carinthia, Carniola).

1279   Statute of *Mortmain* (' Dead Hand ') in England—to check the bestowal of estates on religious foundations— forecasts the beginning of an ebb in monastic enthusiasm.

1280   Death of *Albertus Magnus*, Count of Bollstädt, Bishop of Ratisbon, greatest of German Schoolmen ('Doctor Universalis'), also an architect and a pioneer of natural science. He is supreme in the thirteenth century as an interpreter of Aristotle : in this he was largely guided by the translations and notes of the Arabic commentators. His (?) plans for the completion of Cologne Cathedral have been carried out in the nineteenth century. His position in chemistry and physical geography is noteworthy.

1280–90   Completion of the main part of Strassburg Cathedral (façade by Erwin von Steinbach).

1280   Completion of the ' Angel Choir ', Lincoln Cathedral.

1280   Commencement of the present Cathedral of Orvieto— one of the finest Gothic monuments of Italy.

Sicilian Vespers. Revolt of Sicily against French rule **1282** (Charles of Anjou, King of the Two Sicilies). All French in the island slaughtered at and after vesper-time on Easter Monday, 1282. Sicily joins Aragon.

Completion of *English conquest of Wales*.   **1282–4**

Conquest of Old Prussia by the Teutonic Order practically **1283** completed.

Commencement (by Edward I of England) of Carnarvon **1283** Castle, ' one of the most extensive and imposing of the mediaeval fortresses of Europe '.

The *General Privilege* of Aragon granted. [' The Magna **1283** Carta of Aragon, and perhaps more full and satisfactory than our own.'—Hallam.]

Conway Castle ('perhaps the most beautiful in Wales ') **1284** built by Edward I.

Philip IV (' Le Bel ', ' The Fair ') of France. French **1285–** ascendancy still further advanced by this subtle states- **1314** man, who humbles the Papacy [1303], calls the first National Assembly of France [1302], destroys the Templars [1307– 12], begins the aggrandizement of France in Burgundy [1310, &c.], nearly absorbs French Flanders and the remainder of the King of England's continental dominion.

Completion of the Cathedral of Amiens.   **1288**

Public clock at Westminster.   **1288**

The county of Burgundy ('Frei-Grafschaft ', 'Franche- **1289** Comté ') united for a time with the German kingdom. Provence and Avignon remain in the possession of Charles of Anjou.

Expulsion of the Jews from England by Edward I. **1290** (They are not officially readmitted till Cromwell.)

University of Lisbon.   **1290**

Edward I of England presses Scotland to a political **1290–5** union with England.

1291   First (unsuccessful) attempt (by the Genoese) to find the sea-way round Africa to India. Discovery of a small part of the unknown W. coast of Africa (opposite the Canaries). This anticipates the great maritime expansion (the Oceanic Age) of Europe : progress is very slow till the fifteenth century.

1291   Fall of Acre. Destruction of the last remains of the Crusading States in Syria.

1291   First Roman Catholic Missions in India, founded by the Franciscan John of Monte Corvino, on his way to China and the court of the Grand Khan (Mongol-Chinese Emperor).

1291   League of the Forest Cantons (Uri, Schweiz, Unterwalden), the nucleus of the Swiss Confederation.

1293   First Roman Catholic Missions in China, founded by Monte Corvino, first Roman Bishop of Peking.

1294   Death of Roger Bacon, ' Doctor Mirabilis ', the greatest Christian ' man of science ' before the fifteenth century. (In his later years he describes the composition of a telescope, lenses, an air-pump, gunpowder, &c.) His work in optics, mathematics, geography, philology, grammar, criticism, &c.

1294   First alliance of Scotland with France against England.

1294   Lübeck recognized as head of the Hanseatic League.

1294   Election of Pope Boniface VIII. Guided by his extravagant and unskilful statesmanship, the Papacy comes into fatal conflict with the growing force of nationality, especially as represented by France and England.

1295   The (present) Belfry of Bruges commenced.

1295   Marco Polo and his relatives return to Venice from China (where they had resided from 1275 to 1292 in the service of Kublai Khan).

1295   **Complete National Representative Assembly in England— ' the Model Parliament '** of Edward I. Representation of counties, towns, and lower clergy, united with nobles and prelates. 'That which touches all shall be approved by all.' See 1265, 1275.

Work on the Town Hall of Siena.

1295, &c.

The first English conquest of Scotland. An English viceroy appointed—John, Earl of Warenne, 'guardian of the Kingdom '.

1295–6

Boniface VIII (1294–1303) opens the **last great struggle of the Hildebrandine Papacy with Secular Powers** by the Bull *Clericis Laicos*, forbidding the clergy, and 'religious persons ' of all ranks, to pay taxes to the civil power, without papal permission. Firm action of the French and English Governments in reply to this (e. g. the English clergy, refusing to grant supplies, in obedience to the Bull, are outlawed).

1296

Scottish rising under William Wallace. Victories over the English.

1297

The *Confirmation of the Charters* in England—forced from Edward I by his war with France, the Scottish rising, and the rebellious attitude of the clergy and certain great nobles (e. g. Bohun of Hereford and Bigod of Norfolk).

Commencement of the present (Gothic) Cathedral of Florence.

1298

Marco Polo, in prison at Genoa, writes his book, *Concerning the Kingdoms and Marvels of the East*.

1298

Second English conquest of Scotland. Defeat of Wallace at Falkirk.

1298

Boniface VIII attempts to mediate between France and England.

1298

Boniface VIII claims Papal overlordship in Scotland.

1299

Treaty of Chartres between France and England : Guienne left in possession of the latter. (Philip is especially anxious to have his hands free for dealing with the Papacy and with Flanders : Edward for defence against Church encroachments and for completion of the Scottish conquest.)

1300 *Papal Jubilee at Rome.* Its extraordinary brilliancy (Dante, Giotto, and Villani of Florence are among the visitors to Rome at this time). ' Villani, who was present, says there were always 200,000 strangers in the city during the Jubilee ; another chronicler tells us that it seemed as if an army were marching each way at all hours . . . while Dante draws a simile from the multitudes who passed to and from St. Peter's along the bridge of St. Angelo :

> Even as the Romans, for the mighty host,
> The year of Jubilee, upon the bridge,
> Have chosen a mode to pass the people over. . . .

Offerings were heaped up on the altars. A chronicler tells us that at St. Paul's ("outside the walls") he saw two of the clergy with rakes, employed day and night in "raking together infinite money".' Boniface, intoxicated with the spectacle, renews the struggle with the Secular Powers. (His alleged claims to be 'emperor as well as pope'.) ' The pope was now at the height of his fortune ; while the enthusiasm of the Jubilee filled his Treasury, the veneration of the multitudes ' hailed him as uniting the highest spiritual ' and temporal dominion '.

1300 Growth of the glass-making industry at Venice, and concentration of the manufacture at Murano. The use of glass, both for vessels and windows, by this time is already very general throughout the leading countries of W. Europe.

c. 1300, &c. Progress of paper-making, especially in Italy.

1300 The Italian physician Lanfranchi of Milan writes his *Chirurgia* at Paris, an important era in the history of medicine.

Death of Cimabue of Florence, the first great modern **1300** painter (born *c.* 1240).

[At this time the murder of an Irishman is regarded as **[c. 1300** no offence in the King of England's courts.]

The English king, nobles, and university representatives **1301** repudiate the Pope's claim over Scotland (deduced from the *Donation of Constantine*, or from 'the Princess Scota, daughter of King Pharaoh of Egypt'. The English, of course, rely on 'Brute the Trojan').

Resumption of the Papal quarrel with Philip the Fair. **1301** A new Papal legate of the most provocative type sent into France, Bernard, Bishop of Pamiers. Though a French subject, he declares to Philip himself that he acknowledges no lord but the Pope. Peter Flotte, the French Chancellor, sent to Rome to indict the legate ; Boniface's claims to [supreme] temporal as well as spiritual power ; Flotte's reply, 'Your power is in words ; ours is real'.

The *Four Letters* (*Ausculta, Fili, Salvator Mundi*, &c.) issued by Boniface to assert Papal authority over the king, realm, and Church of France. Prelates and other representatives of the French clergy summoned to a council at Rome for the redress of the grievances of the French Church—'a daring and unprecedented assumption of power over a prince's ecclesiastical subjects '.

Philip defies the Pope, burns *Ausculta, Fili*, and summons **1302** the **First National Representative Assembly of France** (April 1302). The nobles, commons, and even clergy support the king. The French clergy remonstrate with the Pope.

Violent reply of Boniface (*Verba delirantis*) to the French **1302** clergy.

He threatens, in full Consistory, to depose Philip, if contumacious, 'like a groom '.

Defeat of the French by the Flemings at Courtrai **1302**

('Battle of the Spurs'). Philip abandons for the moment his attempt to absorb French Flanders.

Forty-five French prelates, defying the king's authority, set out for the Roman Council [see 1301].

1302   Dante banished from Florence.

1302   At the Roman Council Boniface VIII issues the 'Constitution' *Unam Sanctam,* the *last important document of the Hildebrandine Papacy,* asserting its supremacy over all temporal authority. ('I have set thee over the nations . . . to root out, and to pull down, and to destroy . . . to build and to plant.' 'It is altogether necessary for every human creature to be subject to the Roman Pontiff.')

Philip makes peace with England and the Flemings, abandons the Scottish alliance, restores part of Aquitaine to Edward I.

c. 1302   Commencement of (existing) fortifications of the Kremlin of Old Novgorod, at this time the leading Russian city and one of the largest in Europe.

1303   Philip accuses Boniface of heresy, simony, and other crimes, and calls for his trial before a general council [March].

Excommunication of Philip [April].

Philip *denounces the Inquisition* as inhuman, and offers redress of grievances to every class of his subjects.

The *French National Assembly,* or 'States General', summoned again to Paris, *supports the king,* formulates terrible charges against the Pope, and calls for a general council—the French clergy concurring [June].

Boniface suspends all ecclesiastical elections and university teaching in France [August] and prepares a Bull of Deposition against Philip, to be published on September 8.

Meantime, on September 7, the Pope is *seized at Anagni,* in the Sabine hills, by emissaries and allies of Philip, and roughly treated. He is rescued and brought to Rome,

but dies from the effects of the shock and the 'frenzy
fever' that followed (October 11).

> [I see the Fleur-de-Lys Alagna enter,
> And Christ in his own Vicar captive made ;
> I see him yet another time derided ;
> I see renewed the vinegar and gall,
> And between robbers new I see him slain.
>   Dante, *Purgatorio*, xx.]

**With Boniface VIII ends the great age of the Mediaeval
Papacy.**

['After his failure it never recovered the ascendancy
which he . . . hazarded in the endeavour to gain a yet
more absolute dominion.'—Robertson.]

GENERAL VIEW OF THE STATE OF EUROPE
ABOUT 1303

Decisive changes have occurred since the end of the tenth century (see *General View . . . about* 1000).

1. **Mediaeval civilization has reached its height.** The power and influence of the Church have long been at their height, and all that side of civilization favoured by the Church has brilliantly developed.

The early movements of the New Free Thought (especially in the twelfth century) have been balanced and checked by the progress of Catholic thought. The **thirteenth century** is the noon-time of scholastic, or Catholic, philosophy, the **age of the greatest Catholic thinkers** (such as Aquinas). It also witnesses the **fullest development of the monastic spirit** in the Friars, who depart from the strictly monastic life, evangelize the masses afresh, and rally the spiritual and intellectual energies of Catholicism—in this last point their work resembles that of the Jesuits in the sixteenth century. The **Mediaeval Universities** have arisen, multiplied, and prospered remarkably. The **Organization, Defence, and Doctrine of the Church** have been highly, perhaps injuriously **developed** (as in the thirteenth-century Papacy; in the Inquisition; in the enforcement of Auricular Confession; and in Transubstantiation).

Almost all the **intellectual activities** of the West, even those concerned with natural science, after showing abundant **signs of revolt** in the twelfth, have fallen **more** completely **under Church influence** in the thirteenth century. The Church now adopts Aristotle in full, and is reconciled to such discoveries as that of the magnet in navigation.

The **new literatures** of the West, which begin to show themselves from the eleventh century, are no exception here. The anti-Church spirit of the Troubadours is toned down. This period closes with Dante, the supreme literary artist of Catholicism and of the Imperial Idea. The ecclesiastical **arts,** and especially the **architecture,** of the Middle Ages are in their perfection from the early eleventh century.

The whole of the **material civilization** of Christendom has likewise **developed** remarkably in this central mediaeval time (1000–1300). The **Commercial Republics** of Italy, Flanders, Germany, and other lands are in the heyday of their vigour, prosperity, and influence at the end of the thirteenth century ; while the European **overland expansion** in Asia, developed by the stimulus, or with the alliance, of the Mongol power, brings about a memorable enlargement of our world-knowledge, of European trade, and of Christian missionary activity. These developments are at the root of the oceanic discoveries of later times.

After the crisis of 1303, mediaeval civilization tends to decline—Summer passes into Autumn—while a fresh life grows up (that of the **Classical Renaissance** and the **New Nationalities**) largely hostile to the mediaeval spirit.

2. The **Roman Papacy,** that supreme expression of the mediaeval spirit, shares, of course, to the full in the development of mediaeval life which it has so largely helped to produce. During most of this period (1000–1300) it has really **dominated Western Christendom.** It has **defeated the Western Empire** after a long and desperate struggle (1076–1250). But now it has **itself suffered a decisive defeat in its conflict with** a new force of **Nationality** (1303). This event is the turning-point of the Middle Ages—from mediaeval to modern.

3. Both **Eastern** and **Western Empires** have passed their zenith, and **disastrously declined.** The **Eastern Empire** is **no longer a first-class power,** or an effective bulwark of

Christendom. This is partly the work of Western Crusaders, traitors to Christian interests. The **German kingdom,** on which the Western Empire rests, is **fatally weakened** as a unified state, the leader of Christian nations. But the **German people,** in trade and national expansion, as well as in culture and national civilization, continues to show **remarkable vigour.** The **Hanseatic League** and the **Teutonic Order** are examples of this.

France begins to **take the place of Germany as the leading state** of Europe. The French kingdom as a first-class power is not created till the thirteenth century, when the German kingdom is shattered. But its growth is rapid, and by 1303 it is already near to its commanding position in the seventeenth century. The next age—the mid-fourteenth century—sees a check to this advance, especially through the Hundred Years' War.

England has **lost** the best part of the Anglo-Angevin Empire on the Continent (to the French kingdom), but has **developed** strongly **as an island state,** has made progress towards an Empire of the British Isles, and has worked out a system of Central and Local Government and Justice, which is the chief ancestor of Modern Liberal Constitutions.

Spain has **driven the Muhammadan into a corner** (the kingdom of Granada). Her three chief states, **Castile, Aragon, and Portugal, have taken shape,** and like England have 'organized their liberties'. Aragon begins expansion outside Spain (towards Italy) : the other states will follow.

In **Italy** the **Commercial Republics are at the height of their prosperity** and freedom. They have thriven on the Crusades, have shaken themselves free from the domination of either Empire, and have not yet fallen under their own despots.

Their progress is in many ways imitated, from an early

time in the thirteenth century, by the trading cities of the North, especially in Flanders and Germany.

Hungary, Poland, the *Scandinavian States,* have all become settled members of the European and Catholic family, and have maintained a fairly prosperous national life. The Scandinavians from the eleventh century have gradually lost their ubiquitous expansive energy. Hungary and Poland have both been limited by the German kingdom and the Russian states from a wider growth (till the middle of the thirteenth century).

Russia has enjoyed its highest mediaeval prosperity and strength (in the tenth and eleventh centuries). Its states tend to form an ever-looser federation, and fall a prey to the **Mongols** in the thirteenth century. The old free Russia is almost destroyed, except at Novgorod in the far North. Asiatic Barbarians rule for centuries over the Eastern out-settlements of Europe and Christendom.

The world-empire of these Asiatic Barbarians, the Mongol Tartars (comprising most of Asia and much of Eastern (Russian) Europe), is in many ways the most remarkable political fact at the end of this period. In the thirteenth century it opens most of Asia to European knowledge, trade, and missions.

PERIOD XXIV

FROM THE FALL OF THE HILDEBRANDINE PAPACY AND THE BEGINNING OF THE AVIGNON CAPTIVITY TO THE OUTBREAK OF THE HUNDRED YEARS' WAR, 1303–38

GENERAL POINTS

1. The **Papacy** falls **under French control,** and goes into 'captivity' at Avignon. Degradation of the Roman See. Permanent weakening of its authority. This is the first great proof of the passing away of mediaeval conditions and the mediaeval spirit.

2. **Suppression of the Templars**—another evidence of the decline of mediaeval ideas.

3. **Strength of the French kingdom :** its victories over the Papacy and the Templars; its aggressions on the Empire [Burgundy], on England [possessions in France], on Flanders.

4. **Failure** of the **English attempt** at a complete **empire of the British Isles.** Defeat in Scottish war. Revival of English claims of continental empire.

5. The Swiss Confederation begins to take shape more clearly.

6. Continuance of the **Mongol Empire.** Increased intercourse with Christendom. **European penetration of Asia,** under Mongol protection (especially for trade and mission-work).

7. Progress of **European civilization.** Science, literature, art (architecture, painting, &c.). Dante, Giotto, &c. Earliest scientific maps. Later Gothic style.

Benedict XI, successor to Boniface VIII, releases Philip **1303** of France from excommunication, and annuls all anti-French decrees, sentences, and acts of Boniface (*Clericis Laicos* ' explained '). But Philip still presses for the condemnation of Boniface VIII as a heretic and criminal.

Fresh rising of the Scots and renewed English invasion. **1303** Edward overruns all Scotland. Wallace captured (executed 1305).

Completion of the Cloth Hall at Ypres (begun 1200), **1304** ' the most considerable monument of old Flemish trade in existence '.

Birth of Petrarch (Francesco Petrarca). **1304**

University of Orleans (really dating from 1230 to 1250, **1305** and, in the form of ' Schools ', especially of classical learning, reaching back to the earlier Middle Ages) extended and incorporated by Pope Clement V. It becomes one of the chief legal Schools of Europe.

University of Lisbon moved to Coimbra, its permanent **1305** home.

The Archbishop of Bordeaux, elected Pope as Clement V, **1305** comes to terms with Philip, and **moves** the seat of **the Papacy to France or the Franco-Burgundian border,** being crowned at Lyons, residing for the next four years in various parts of France, and finally settling at **Avignon** (1309), close to, but just beyond, the frontier of the French kingdom. The Papacy now becomes thoroughly French for the next seventy years, the period of the ' **Babylonish Captivity** ', 1305–76/7. During this time it is, in great measure, an instrument of the French Crown.

Robert Bruce murders ' the Red Comyn ', and leads **1306** a fresh Scottish rising against English rule. He is crowned at Scone. Fresh English invasion of Scotland. Bruce defeated.

1307   Philip of France arranges with the Papacy the *suppression of the Templars*, on condition of dropping his attack on the memory of Boniface VIII. All Templars in France (and, soon after, in the other countries of Roman Christendom) are arrested, imprisoned, and examined on charges of heresy, apostasy, and immorality.

> I see the novel Pilate so relentless—
> This [1] does not sate him—but without decretal
> He to the Temple bears his sordid sails.
> Dante, Purgatorio, xx.

1307   *Death of* **Edward I** *of England.*   His notable work in English political and constitutional development. Revival of the cause of Scottish independence.

   The English Parliament at Carlisle asks for legislation against various Papal taxes and privileges (e. g. Papal ' provision ' of benefices : see 1351, 1390).

1307   (The traditional *Oath on the Rütli*, in the legend of the Swiss Liberators, belongs to this year.)

1308   Baronial uprisings against the misgovernment of Edward II, and especially against the favourite, Piers Gaveston.

1308   Death of Duns Scotus, one of the chief Schoolmen of the later Middle Ages, ' Doctor Subtilis '. A critic of Thomas Aquinas. A leading teacher, first at Oxford, then at Paris.

1309   The Emperor Henry VII recognizes the immediate dependence of the Swiss Forest Cantons (Uri, Schwyz, Unterwalden) upon the Empire, thus supporting their claim to be independent of the Hapsburg counts and other lords.

1309   Beginning of the *Papal residence* (' *captivity* ') *at Avignon.*

1309   Seat of the Grand-Master of the *Teutonic Order* (first at

---

[1] The overthrow of Boniface VIII.

Acre ; at Venice after the fall of Acre, 1291–1309) transferred to Marienburg in W. Prussia, SE. of Danzig.
Highest development of the power of the order at this time
and during the next hundred years. Buildings of the
knights at Marienburg.

Edward II of England put under baronial control **1310**
(twenty-one peers and bishops to regulate the realm and
royal household, under the name of *Lords Ordainers*).

The **Council of Ten** formed **at Venice** for suppression of **1310**
conspiracies against the Republic.

Expedition of the Emperor Henry VII to Rome and **1310–13**
Italy (celebrated by Dante). He is crowned King of Italy
at Pavia, Emperor at Rome (1312), subdues Brescia, is
welcomed in Genoa and Pisa, repulsed from Florence, dies
on his way to attack Naples (1313).

Beginning of the rule of the *Visconti in Milan* (as gover- **1310**
nors for the Emperor Henry VII).

Annexation of Lyons to France by Philip the Fair. **1310–12**
The county of Burgundy ['Frei-Grafschaft', 'Franche-
Comté', an imperial possession since 1033, q. v.], momentarily gained by France (marriage of Philip IV).
With this **begins French aggression at the expense of
other powers,** and in particular at the expense of the old
kingdom of Burgundy.

Progress of the cause of Scottish independence under **1311–13**
Robert Bruce (Perth taken 1312 ; Edinburgh, 1313).

Suppression of the Templars in France, and throughout **1312**
Roman Christendom, by Papal Bull.

Fresh English invasion of Scotland, repulsed in battle **1314**
of **Bannockburn,** which decisively **secures** the **independence
of the Scots.**

Death of **Philip the Fair.** His great work for the con- **1314**
solidation and extension of the French kingdom (develop-

ment of the French Parliament ; aggression on the fiefs of England ; annexation of Lyons ; aggression on the Empire ; the welding together of the French nation in the struggle with the Papacy). Philip's position as leader of the new nations in the struggle of the secular power against the Papal claims. His anticipations of future anti-Church movement—as in the overthrow of Boniface VIII, the subjection of the Papacy to French domination, the dissolution of the Templars.

1314–30   New interregnum in Germany, through a disputed election (Lewis the Bavarian ; Frederick of Austria).

1315–18   Scotch attack on Ireland under Edward and Robert Bruce. Remarkable initial success is followed by failure.

1315   *Battle of Morgarten.* Victory of the Swiss Confederates over Leopold of Austria. Ludwig the Bavarian renews the recognition of the immediate dependence of the Forest Cantons upon the Empire.

1315   Death of Raymond Lull ['Lully'], Spanish noble, schoolman, and missionary [b. 1235 at Palma, Majorca]. His *Ars Magna*—an attempt at a new method of investigation in knowledge, adapted to 'answer any question or any topic'. Lull's voluminous works contain many points of interest—e.g. on the map-science and navigation of that time, and on the possibility of discovering an all-sea route round Africa to the Indies.

1318   Invasion of the North of England by the Scots under Robert Bruce. Wasting of Yorkshire.

1320   Beginnings of the University of Florence.

c. 1320   *Cracow becomes the capital of Poland* (and so remains till c. 1550–1609, when the seat of government is gradually moved to Warsaw. It remains the coronation city till the eve of the ruin of Poland—1764). In earlier time (from the eleventh century) Gnesen had perhaps more nearly occupied the position of a capital than any other Polish town.

Fierce quarrels of the Papacy (especially under John XXII) **1320–9** with the extreme or ' Spiritual Franciscans ' (' Fraticelli '), who demanded ' evangelic poverty' of the Pope and all churchmen, denounced the wealth, splendour, and luxury of the Papal Court and so much of the hierarchy, and in some ways prepared the way for Wycliffism. The learned Fraticelli, such as William of Occam, pursued lines of thought far from helpful to Papal claims, while itinerant friar-preachers ' familiarized the people down to the lowest classes with the notion that the Pope and the [local] Roman Church were the mystical Antichrist and Babylon '. Thus 'the surest support of the Papacy was turned in great part to dangerous opposition '.

Death of Dante Alighieri, greatest of mediaeval and of **1321** all Italian poets ; one of the chief names in literature. The *Divina Commedia* (*Inferno, Purgatorio, Paradiso*), probably begun before 1300, was mainly written before 1318, while Dante was in exile. His *De Monarchia* ' the epitaph of the Mediaeval State '.

The English House of Commons finally gains a share **1322** in legislation, and the wages of the members are fixed.

The unique lantern of Ely Cathedral, the only Gothic **1322–8** dome in England, built.

Marsilio of Padua issues his *Defensor Pacis*, a ' prediction **1326** of the Modern State ', which questions the extreme Papal claims, both temporal and spiritual [see 1349].

Completion of the Town Hall of Siena [see 1295].   **1327**

The *Ottoman Turks* take Brusa, and begin to be an **1327** *important power in Asia Minor.*

Birth of Geoffrey **Chaucer,** the first great English poet, **c. 1328** one of the leading figures in the new literatures of Europe.

1328   Complete independence of Scotland recognized by England.

1325–41   Ivan 'Kalita' ['Purser'] **founds** the **greatness of Moscow,** largely by his eager and efficient subservience to his Mongol overlords. To Moscow is now permanently attached (except for very rare intervals) (*a*) the Grand Princedom or political headship of the Russian principalities ; (*b*) the Metropolitan or spiritual head of the Russian Church.

1329   Death of ' Meister ' Eckhart, German religious teacher, earliest of the great speculative mystics, pupil (?) of Albert the Great, teacher of Tauler [see 1361].

1332–3   Separation of the Houses of Lords and Commons in the English Parliament.

1334   Death of Giotto of Florence, architect and painter, ' the true father of modern painting '

1337   Edward III of England raises his claim to the French throne.

1338   **Outbreak of the Hundred Years' War.**

1338   The Electors of the Empire (at Rhense, near Coblenz) declare the Papal coronation unnecessary for the complete recognition of an Emperor.

Before 1338   **Gunpowder** was probably invented before this time : it is first used about 1340, q. v.

PERIOD XXV

FROM THE OUTBREAK OF THE HUNDRED YEARS' WAR TO THE END OF THE PAPAL CAPTIVITY AT AVIGNON, 1338–78

GENERAL POINTS

1. First period of the **Hundred Years' War** between France and England. English victories and conquests, followed by loss of almost all acquisitions. Development of French power long delayed by this war.

2. The **Papal ' captivity ' at Avignon** continued ; it is at last ended by return to Rome. Struggles of French influence to retain ascendancy.

2 *a*. Largely through the Avignon scandal, **anti-Papal and anti-Church views revive,** especially through John Wycliffe, ' the forerunner of Protestantism in England '.

3. The **Black Death** sweeps over all Europe, producing decisive economic and social changes (peasant revolts, &c.).

4. Further decline of the Eastern Empire. The Ottoman **Turks in Europe :** their pressure upon Constantinople.

5. Partial improvement in the power of the Western Empire and German kingdom. Prosperity of German trade and city life (**Hanseatic League**) and of German racial expansion (**Teutonic Order,** &c.) Growth of the **Swiss** or High German League.

6. Progress of European **explorations** in the Atlantic and in Asia—prosecution of trade, missions, &c., in the Mongol world.

6 *a*. End of the Mongol world-empire.   Collapse of European trade, missions, &c., in Asia.

7. Developments of **European civilization.**   Literature, art, science, &c.   First use of *gunpowder*.   New universities.   Decline of *scholasticism*.   Growth of *mysticism*, early *Protestantism*.   First signs of the **Classical Renaissance.**

Outbreak of war between France and England.   **1338**

Embassy (headed by the Franciscan, John de Marignolli) **1338–53**
sent to the Mongol courts, and especially to that of the
supreme Mongol-Chinese emperor in Peking, from the Pope.

First appearance of any of the African islands (some of **1339**
Canaries, and perhaps Madeiras) in modern scientific maps.

Naval victory of the English and their Flemish allies **1340**
(the latter inspired by James van Artevelde, the ' tribune '
of Ghent) at Sluys.

Monastery of the Trinity (' Troitsa ') founded near **1340**
Moscow—after Kiev the richest, most celebrated, and
most important religious house of Russia, centre of the
national resistance to the Poles in the early seventeenth
century (1608, &c.).

The invasion of Spain by fresh Muslim hosts from Africa **1340**
(Berbers) defeated at the battle of Tarifa, or the Salado
(' Salt Stream '). **One of the first recorded instances of fire-
arms.**

Exploration of the Canaries by a Portuguese fleet with **1341**
Italian pilots and captains. This expedition is described
by Boccaccio.

Powerful position of the Magyar state (Hungary) at **1342–82**
this time, under King Lewis ' the Great '. Conquest of
Moldavia. Defeat of Bulgaria and Venice. Temporary
union of Hungary and Poland [see 1370].

Buildings of Edward III of England at Windsor Castle, **c. 1344,**
largely reconstructions of the work of William the Con- **&c.**
queror, Henry III, &c.

Foundation of the University of Valladolid.   **1346**

Voyage of Catalan adventurers to West Africa. Dis- **1346**
covery of fresh coast (from Cape Nun to Cape Bojador)
opposite the Canaries.

1346   English invasion of N. France.   Great English victory at Crécy in Picardy.   Use of little cannon.

1347–54   Cola di Rienzi attempts the ' fantastic enterprise ' of a ' restoration of the Roman Republic '.   Transient, brilliant success, followed by failure.

1347   Siege and capture of Calais by the English.

1347–8   The **Black Death,** the most terrible of recorded pestilences, reaches France, Italy, England, Spain, and Germany, 1348.   It perhaps originated in China : it is noticed in Russia and the Crimea, in Armenia and Asia Minor, on its way westward.   It continues to ravage most of Europe at intervals, till about 1368–9, and helps to produce great economic and social change.

1347–9   Acquisition of Montpellier (from Aragon), and of *Dauphiné*, by the French kingdom.   From this the heir of the French crown acquires the title of *Dauphin*.

1347   First imposition of the *Gabelle* tax (an impost on salt) in France..

1348   Foundation of the *University of Prague*, the earliest in Central Europe, by Charles IV, Emperor and King of Bohemia (' Bohemia's father, the Empire's stepfather ').

1349   Death of Richard Rolle of Hampole, saint, ascetic, and preacher, author of *The Prick of Conscience* and other works important in the development of (Middle) English language and literature.

1349   *Ordinance of Labourers* in England, fixing wages, forbidding alms to ' sturdy beggars ', &c.

c. 1349   Death of *William of Occam*, ' Doctor invincibilis ', the most brilliant of the schoolmen of the fourteenth century. He represents also the anti-Papal tendencies of the Franciscan revolt of this time.   Protected by the Emperor Ludwig (Louis) of Bavaria, he writes against the more extreme Papal claims, both temporal and spiritual. He is said to have inspired Marsilio of Padua : see 1326, 1320–9.

Spire of Salisbury Cathedral finished.   **1350**

Nave of Glasgow Cathedral built.   **1350**

Finishing work to Notre-Dame, Paris.   **1351**

The great Genoese (?) Atlas, known as the *Laurentian* **1351** *Portolano*, shows knowledge already acquired by Italian (and Portuguese) mariners, &c., of the African Islands (Canaries, Madeiras, Azores), and somewhat anticipates correct ideas on the shape of the African continent. Good knowledge of W. Asia, of the whole Mediterranean, the Euxine, and the West Coast of Europe, up to Flanders, also shown.

First *Statute of Provisors* in England, to prevent exercise **1351** of Papal patronage in the English Church [see 1307, 1390].

First Statute of Treasons in England.   **1352**

The present Antwerp Cathedral ('largest and most **1352** beautiful Gothic church in the Netherlands') commenced.

First *Statute of Praemunire* in England—against appeals **1353** to foreign (i.e. Papal) courts.

Development of the *Swiss Confederacy*, by inclusion of **1353** all the eight old cantons (Uri, Schwyz, Unterwalden, Luzern, Zürich, Zug, Glarus, Bern).

English victory at Poitiers. Capture of the French king, **1356** John II. Terrible sufferings of France, especially of the poorer classes, from the war. *Revolutionary movements* in town and country.

(*a*) Rising in *Paris*, under Étienne Marcel, ' provost of **1357–8** the merchants ', who from 1355 had been one of the leaders of the commons, and (after Poitiers) a leader in the fortification and defence of the French capital. Marcel becomes, for a time, master of the city. He allies himself with the revolted peasantry (*Jacquerie*), establishes a momentary

'Parliamentary Government', but is killed July 1358.
(The French Revolution treated him as a forerunner.)

1358   (*b*) The *Jacquerie*, a rising of the French *peasantry*—
mainly in the NE. near Beauvais, Compiègne, Senlis,
Amiens—accompanied by, and suppressed with, great
cruelty, May–June 1358.

1356–8   First establishment of the **Ottoman Turks in Europe**—
crossing of the Dardanelles, seizure of Gallipoli, &c.
From this time the ruin of Christian Constantinople and
of the relics of the Eastern Empire is clearly threatened.

1356   The *Golden Bull*, or (revised) fundamental law of the
Empire issued by the Emperor Charles IV.

The *Electoral College of the Holy Roman Empire now
finally fixed.*   Seven Electors, three clerical, four lay :
(1) Archbishop of Mainz, arch-chancellor of Germany ;
(2) Archbishop of Trier (Trèves), arch-chancellor of
Italy ; (3) Archbishop of Cologne, arch-chancellor of Burgundy ; (4) King of Bohemia, arch-seneschal ; (5) Count
Palatine of the Rhine, arch-steward ; (6) Duke of Saxony
('Sachsen-Wittenberg' line), arch-marshal; (7) Margrave of
Brandenburg, arch-chamberlain. (Note. The electoral vote
is now refused to Bavaria, though this had been one of
the four great duchies of the earliest days of the German
kingdom : see above, under Henry the Fowler, p. 74.)

The states of these Electors are declared to be indivisible
and inalienable ; and the electoral vote is attached to the
holder of the land in each case.

from c.
1350 to
1360
About this time the **Hanseatic League** arrives at its
highest power, and assumes its full organization.   Nearly
a hundred cities (including many inland) now belong to
it, from Holland and Zealand to the Gulf of Finland.   Lübeck
becomes recognized as the leading city of the whole League.
Various divisions of the League : by about 1400 we have :—
(*a*) *Wendish and Pomeranian*, including the primary cities

of Lübeck and Hamburg ; and the less important, but flourishing, ports of the South Baltic coast, and of Holstein, from the mouth of the Elbe, and Kiel, to Rügen Island, Stettin, and the beginning of Prussia ; (*b*) *Saxon*, including Bremen, Magdeburg, and Brunswick ; also Goslar, Hanover, Göttingen, Halle, &c. ; (*c*) *Prussian*, including Danzig, Königsberg, Elbing, Marienburg, Thorn, &c. ; (*d*) *Westphalian*, including Cologne, Münster, &c., and all the present German industrial region of the lower Rhine, and from the Rhine east to the Weser ; (*e*) *Margravian* (i.e. Brandenburg), including Brandenburg and Berlin ; (*f*) *Netherland*, including various Dutch cities ; (*g*) *Livonian*, including various Baltic coast-towns from the present frontier of Russia and Germany almost to the mouth of the Neva and the site of St. Petersburg, to which we may add the islands of Gothland (with Wisby town, once the centre of the League) and Öland, off the Swedish coast.

Not only the head-centres of the Hansa [Lübeck, Bremen, Hamburg, &c.], but also several of the less-known members of the League, e.g. Wismar, Rostock, Stralsund, Greifswald, Stargard, had remarkable commercial life at this time. And in many of them interesting monuments of this mercantile prosperity survive.

The League had immense interests in foreign countries (by the end of the fourteenth century it dominated the trade of all Northern Europe). It maintained many organized, often more or less fortified, trading-stations in various non-German towns. The chief of these were— (1) London in England (*The Steel-Yard* was here the name of the Hansa factory) ; (2) Bruges in Old French Flanders ; (3) Bergen in Norway ; (4) Novgorod in Russia. To which may be added (5) Wisby in Gothland, after this island ceases to be considered as a piece of Hanseatic and German territory.

Spread of the Hansa in the Baltic, in thirteenth and

fourteenth centuries, aided by the power of the Teutonic Order at this time (holding S. and E. Baltic coasts, from Danzig to the Gulf of Finland).

Remarkable activity of *German colonization in the Baltic,* especially in thirteenth and fourteenth centuries—compare Greek, Italian, and Russian colonization in the Black Sea in ancient, mediaeval, and modern times.

1360   *Peace of Brétigny* between France and England. Cession of Aquitaine (including Gascony, Guyenne, Poitou, and all SW. of France), together with Calais, &c., to England. Edward III renounces his claim on the French throne.

1361,   About this time a terrible recurrence of the Black Death,
&c.   especially in England.

Revolutionary tendencies among lower English classes [as among French : see 1356]. Preaching of John Ball.

1361   Death of Johann Tauler, the Dominican, of Strassburg and Basel, a great religious teacher, chief among the German mystics and preachers of the Middle Ages [see 1329].

c. 1361   About this time English once more begins to be the regular language of the English Law Courts, as for some years of the English boys' schools ; and trial by jury assumes more modern form.

1361-2   The Ottoman Turks take Adrianople and Philippopolis. Constantinople is now surrounded by Turkish power and territory.

1361-2,   First great war of the Hanseatic League with Walde-
&c.   mar III of Denmark. Copenhagen taken and plundered by the forces of the League under John Wittenborg, burgomaster of Lübeck. Wittenborg, defeated off Helsingborg, is disgraced, imprisoned, and executed at Lübeck.

1362   *The Vision of William concerning Piers the Plowman,* an English poem of real genius, giving a dark picture of

fourteenth-century life in England, first written by William
Langland (or Langley)—revised and enlarged about 1377.

Alleged voyages of French sailors, especially from **c. 1364,**
Normandy [Dieppe, Rouen], to the Guinea coast, beyond **&c.**
C. Verde (?).

First foundation of the University of Cracow [see 1401]. **1364**

First foundation of the University of Vienna.   **1364**

Congress of the Hanseatic League at Cologne (repre- **1364**
sentatives from seventy-seven towns). Promulgation of
a constitution, and declaration of war against Denmark.

William of Wykeham, Bishop of Winchester—one of **1366–**
the chief English mediaeval statesmen, churchmen, and **1404**
builders. His work in the Good Parliament [see 1376] ;
in the foundation of Winchester College, and of New College,
Oxford ; and in the rebuilding of Winchester Cathedral.

Second (wholly victorious) war of the Hansa with **1367–70**
Denmark. Flight of Waldemar. By Treaty of Stralsund,
1370, the League imposes humiliating terms on Denmark,
and secures enormous advantages (domination of *the
Sound*, and, for a time, of Scania, thus controlling the
entrance of the Baltic ; claim to a voice in the succession
to the Danish crown). Thus the *Hansa arrives at its full
development.* ' La Ligue va atteindre l'âge viril ' (Worms).

Till the sixteenth century the Hansa retains its commercial ascendancy over the Scandinavian lands. But
much of its political power passes with the Union of
Kalmar (1397).

Other leagues in Germany, somewhat similar to, and
sometimes overlapping, the Northern Hansa, may be
noticed, e. g. (1) the *Rhine League*, founded 1254 by the
confederating of Mainz and Worms in the time of the
Great Interregnum, joined by the Archbishops of Mainz,
Cologne, Trier, and other bishops, nobles, and cities, and

several times renewed ; in 1381 united with (2) the *Swabian City League,* founded 1331, renewed 1376.

Modern German commercial and maritime activity is foreshadowed and illustrated by the Hansa and the other city leagues of this time.

1368–70   **Break-up of the Mongol Empire.** Expulsion of the Mongols from China. Collapse of Christian trade, missions, &c., throughout the Mongol world.

1369   The Bastille (or fort at the gate of St. Antoine), Paris, completed by Charles V of France. From the first it is a state-prison as well as a fortress, and the former use becomes ultimately the chief characteristic of this vast and gloomy pile, destroyed July 14, 1789.

1369–74   Renewal of the Hundred Years' War between England and France. *Loss of* all the *English gains* (of the Brétigny Treaty), except Calais. English Aquitaine again restricted to Bordeaux, Bayonne, and the coastal strip. Truce.

1369   **Timur** [Timur Lenk, ' Tamerlane '] begins to build up a second Mongol Empire in Western and Central Asia.

1370   Temporary union of the crowns of Hungary and Poland under Lewis ' the Great ' of Hungary [see 1342–82].

c. 1373   Beginnings of the Royal Library of France under Charles V (first catalogue, 1373). This collection was, however, taken to England after 1425 and dispersed [see 1440–53].

1373   William of Wykeham, Bishop of Winchester, begins the foundation of Winchester College, the oldest of the great public schools of England.

1375   Death of **Boccaccio** (b. 1313), the first great European novelist, author of the *Decameron* ; one of the founders, with Dante and Petrarch, of modern Italian as a literary language ; and, with Petrarch, one of the chief harbingers of the Classical Renaissance.

The Catalan Atlas (giving the best representation of **1375**
Asia—especially of the Indian Peninsula and the Chinese
Orient, here first delineated with some accuracy—that
had yet appeared). ' Here we have much the same picture
of a Far East and the Indies that Marco Polo himself would
have drawn, if he had turned cartographer.'

Death of Orcagna, after Giotto the leading Italian **1376 (?)**
painter, sculptor, and architect of the fourteenth century
(b. 1316 ?).   Magnificent works at Florence, Orvieto
(Pisa ?), &c.

The *Good Parliament* in England.   Attack upon royal **1376**
favourites.   Parliament—supported by the Black Prince
and William of Wykeham, Bishop of Winchester—begins
to exercise the power of *impeachment*.   John of Gaunt,
fourth son of Edward III, who had been practically at
the head of the ' government by favourites ', is momentarily driven from power, but recovers it after the dissolution of the Good Parliament and the death of the Black
Prince (June 1376).

John Wycliffe, supported by John of Gaunt, begins to
attack the clergy and the religious orders.

Pope Gregory XI, urged from many quarters—some **1376-7**
represented by Petrarch, others by St. Catherine of Siena
and other prophetesses of this time—leaves Avignon
(Sept.) and **returns to Rome** (January).   **End of the ' Babylonish captivity '** of the Papacy.

Poll-tax in England.   Death of Edward III.   Accession **1377**
of his grandson, Richard II.

Commencement of the (present) 'Cathedral' of Ulm in **1377**
Württemberg, with designs for the loftiest spire in Christendom, 534 feet, carried out in nineteenth century.

Death of Gregory XI at Rome (March).   **1378**
Struggle of conflicting interests—French and Italian
especially—for control of the Papacy.

PERIOD XXVI

FROM THE OUTBREAK OF THE GREAT SCHISM TO THE COUNCIL OF CONSTANCE, 1378-1415

GENERAL POINTS

1. The **Great Schism.** French influence at the Papal Court, defeated by the return from Avignon, revives in the *Schism* (rival lines of French and Italian popes).

2. Progress of ' Wycliffism ' in England, and of parallel ' Hussite ' movements in Bohemia. This ' **early Protestantism** ' is checked by a strong alliance of Church and State in the countries affected (Wycliffism is somewhat allied to the ' social revolution ' and extreme democratic tendencies). Persecution of ' Lollards '.

The **Council of Constance** meets to end the Schism, put down Wycliffism and Hussism, and reform the Church.

3. Highest development of the English **Parliament** and of English **Constitutional Liberties** in the Middle Ages. Limitations of the Monarchy, especially under the first Lancastrian king.

Social and economic changes in England. The peasant revolt of 1381.

4. Decisive **struggle of Genoa and Venice,** ended by the victory of Venice, which from this time eclipses her rival. Rapid decline of Genoa.

Rise of **Florence.**

Growth of the power of the Tyrants in Italy. Ruin of most of the City-Republics.

5. Beginnings of the great age of **Portugal.**

6. The **union of Poland and Lithuania.**
Defeat of the Teutonic Order by Poland-Lithuania.
Ebb of German colonization and conquest in Eastern
Europe.

7. Moscow begins to lead a movement of **Russian inde-pendence** and nationality against the Tartars. Brilliant
success, followed by disaster.

8. Continued decay of the Eastern Empire.
Progress of **Turkish power.** Conquest of most of Balkan
Peninsula. Imminent danger of Constantinople, post-
poned by

9. Rise of a **Second Mongol Empire,** that **of Timur,** which
defeats the Ottoman Turks and the Golden Horde (thus
helping Constantinople and Russia), but dissolves at the
death of Timur.

10. The **Union of Kalmar** joins Denmark, Norway, and
Sweden in one great united kingdom, for a time.

11. Progress of **European civilization.** Beginnings of
Perpendicular architecture (last phase of Gothic). Last
age of Scholasticism. Growth of Mysticism.

New Universities. Literature, science, and art. Growing
strength of classical ' Renaissance ' movements.

1378– Rebuilding of nave and transepts of Canterbury Cathedral
1414 in present ' Perpendicular ' form.

1378 Accession of Pope Urban VI, an Italian. His extreme
personal unpopularity, and the strength of the French
party in the College of Cardinals, cause the outbreak of
the **Great Schism** (September 1378), which lasts till 1415.
Two lines of popes, an Italian and a French, both claim
recognition ; from 1410 to 1415 a third line appears, as
the only result of the efforts of the Council of Pisa to end
the Schism.

From this time the *popes begin to reside at the Vatican*
Palace : up to the Avignon captivity they usually kept
their court at the Lateran.

1378 The ' Strassburg clock ' constructed.

1379 Foundation of New College, Oxford, by William of
Wykeham, Bishop of Winchester.

1379–80 Poll-taxes in England. Popular discontent.

1379 ' Bills of exchange ' first recognized in English law.

1380 Completion of the buildings of Charles V of France
(begun 1364) at the Royal Palace of the Louvre, Paris.

1380 Death of Charles V of France (' le Sage '). Accession
of the child-king, Charles VI, whose insanity soon declares
itself (from 1392).

c. 1380 *Wycliffe* completes and *issues his translation of the Bible*
—the earliest version in English of the whole of Old and
New Testaments.

1381 The ' Peasant Revolt ', in England—' the English Jacquerie '—led by Wat Tyler, Jack Straw, John Ball, &c.,
aided by Wycliffe's teaching and the preaching of his
' Poor Priests '. London in the hands of the insurgents.
Murder of Archbishop Sudbury of Canterbury in the Tower.
The palace of the Savoy sacked, with other great residences
in town and country. Abolition of villeinage demanded

(and promised by Richard II). Most of the insurgents disperse. Wat Tyler killed. The revolt suppressed. Measures of retaliation, as in France.

Both in England and in France these risings help reactionary tendencies, which culminate in the age of the New Monarchies. In England the rising of 1381 also helps to hasten the end of villeinage.

The **Peace of Turin** ends the ' war of Chioggia ' between **1381** Venice and Genoa. From this time Genoa rapidly declines, and Venice gains the undisputed primacy among commercial republics and Italian naval powers.

The democracy of Ghent, long led by James and Philip **1382** van Artevelde, defeated by the French forces at Roosebeke, where Philip van Artevelde is killed. James, his father, had been murdered in 1345.

Death of John Wycliffe. In his last years (especially **1384** in his *Trialogus*, 1383-4) he parts more and more clearly from the accepted theology of the West. Thus, e.g., he speaks of the Pope as 'the great Antichrist', of the chief prelates as ' lesser Antichrists ' ; denounces indulgences and the position of the ' saints ' in the Church system ; expounds a doctrine of the Eucharist which is practically ' virtualism ' ; denies the necessity of episcopacy ; and attacks confession and the whole penitential system, extreme unction, &c. The endowments of the Church, the orders of monks and friars, and even the mass of the clergy, he attacks, much in the manner of the later Protestants.

Wycliffe is historically the **first great teacher of ' Protestantism '.** Through Lollards and Hussites his views are kept alive into the sixteenth century.

The *Canterbury Tales* of Chaucer.   **1384-8**

Foundation of the University of Heidelberg.   **1385**

By this time the power of the Ottoman Turks is estab- **1385** lished over most of Bulgaria and Macedonia. Danger of Constantinople.

1385   Accession of John the Great, founder of the *House of Aviz*, to the throne of Portugal. Repulse of the Castillian invasion (August 14, 1385, battle of Aljubarrota, north of Lisbon ; decisive victory of Portugal). With this begins the **importance of Portugal** to the world. From 1415 till 1492 Portugal is the leader of the European expansion, and till about 1580 she remains, with Spain, the chief colonial power.

1386   Important victory of the Swiss Confederates at Sempach over Leopold of Austria, in alliance with the south German nobles.

Struggles between the Dukes of Austria and the Swiss Confederates continue, 1385–1468, ending in the success of the latter.

1386   Library of the University of Heidelberg established (oldest still existing in Germany ?).

1386   **Union of Poland and Lithuania** by the marriage of the Polish Queen Hedwig [Yatviga] with the Lithuanian Grand Prince Yagielo ('Jagellon'), and the **conversion of Lithuania** to Christianity ('Jagellon' dynasty, 1386–1572).

1387   Commencement of Milan Cathedral.

1388   Foundation of the Church and Monastery of Batalha in Portugal (the finest Gothic building in that country) in commemoration of the victory of 1385 [which see].

1388,   Struggles between the nobles and the cities in South
&c.   Germany.

1388   Foundation of the University of Cologne.

1389   Great victory of the Ottomans over the Serbs, and their allies, at **Kossovo** Polye. This marks the complete subjection of the Slavs of the Balkan Peninsula by the Turks.

Timur attacks and defeats the Mongols of Russia ('the **1390** Golden Horde'), thereby helping towards the ultimate **&c.** emancipation of Christian Russia from the Tartars (completed by 1480).

Conquests of Timur (Timur Lenk, 'Lame Timur', or **1370-** Tamerlane), who forms a second Mongol Empire in Central **1405** and Western Asia. His terrible devastations, from Delhi to Damascus, from the Aegean to the Volga and the Irtish.

The principal buildings of the Alhambra, Granada, **1390** completed [see 1270].

The re-issued and strengthened Statutes of *Provisors* **1390-3** (1390), *Mortmain* (1391), and *Praemunire* (1393), in England, illustrate the rise of the New Nationalism and the waning political power of the Church.

Foundation of the University of Ferrara by a Bull of **1391** Pope Boniface IX.

Madness of King Charles VI of France. Disputes over **1392** Regency. Civil strife.

Gower's *Confessio Amantis*.   **1393**

Turkish pressure upon Constantinople. But for the **1395-** intervention of Timur, the Ottomans would have become **1402** masters of the city.

A Christian Crusade, led by Sigismund, King of Hungary, **1396** afterwards emperor, to deliver Constantinople and the Balkan lands from the power of the Ottoman Turks, is utterly defeated by Sultan Bajazet (Bayazid) at Nikopolis on the Danube.

John Galeazzo Visconti founds the *Certosa* ('Char- **1396** treuse' or Carthusian House), 'the most sumptuous monastery of Italy', near Pavia.

Bodiam Castle, Sussex, completed—a typical illustra- **c. 1396** tion of the English fortress-mansion of the later Middle Age.

1397, The earliest of the important (existing) buildings of the
&c. Kremlin at Moscow begun (Cathedral of the Annuncia-
tion).

1397 The **Union of Kalmar** [in Sweden] unites all the three
Scandinavian powers, Denmark, Sweden (with Finland),
and Norway, under the sovereignty of Denmark, in the
person of Queen Margaret.

Importance of this Union, which is a parallel to those
of Leon and Castile (1230), Poland and Lithuania (1386),
Castile and Aragon (1479), England and Scotland (1603),
and which offered the Scandinavian nations a unique
opportunity of combining in a really powerful state.
Sweden finally broke away in 1520. Norway and Denmark
remained united till 1814.

After *Oslo* (Old Christiania) becomes the capital of Norway.
1397
1398 John **Hus,** the leading exponent on the Continent of
' **Protestant**' **views** similar to Wycliffe's, becomes a leading figure in Prague—professor at the University, preacher
at Bethlehem Chapel. He is also a champion of **Bohemian
nationalism,** embodied in the Slav or Chekh majority, as
against the powerful German minority.

1399 **Deposition of Richard II of England.** *End of the Plantagenet and beginning of the Lancastrian line. Assertion of
constitutional right* (a parallel, in many ways, to 1688).
Richard's fall is the overthrow of a new absolutism which
had attempted to crush the mediaeval liberties. ' He had
challenged the Constitution, and the Constitution had
broken him.' Henry IV comes in as a constitutional
sovereign, as an ally of the Church against Wycliffism or
Lollardy, and as a defender of Society against revolutionary
doctrine and movement.

Before Completion of the Cathedral of Bourges (some additions
1400 in sixteenth century).

c. 1400 Perpendicular architecture (the last great development of Gothic) begins to prevail in W. Europe. In later fifteenth century it passes into more and more florid forms (called in France *Flamboyant*).

Death of William Langland, author of *Piers Plowman* **1400** [see pp. 180–1].

Conspiracy against the Lancastrian dynasty in England. **1400** Revolt of Owen Glendower in Wales.

Birth of Luca della Robbia, great Florentine artist and **1400** sculptor, especially in terra-cotta (died 1482).

Death of Geoffrey Chaucer [see 1328]. **1400**

Reconstitution and complete foundation of the Uni- **1400–1** versity of Cracow, the earliest in Poland [see 1364].

Fresh interregnum in Germany. **1400–10** Repudiation of Wenzel (Wenceslaus) as emperor by a strong party in Germany (1400). He reigns as King of Bohemia till 1419. Rupert, Count Palatine, 1400–10, the opposition emperor, is almost a figure-head.

Birth of Nicolas of Cusa (d. 1464), sometimes called ' the **1401** last of the schoolmen ', but rather to be classed with the mystics (see Eckhard 1329). The better Scholasticism is now passing into Mysticism.

The Act *De Heretico Comburendo* in England, a result **1401** of the alliance between the Lancastrians and the Church. First executions for Lollard heresy follow.

Timur attacks the Ottoman Turks and defeats them at **1402** Angora, in North-Central Asia Minor (July). Bajazet taken prisoner. All Asia Minor momentarily overrun by Timur's armies. The *Ottoman power broken for twenty years* : the *fall of Constantinople deferred* for half a century.

Seville Cathedral (the present building, perhaps the **1402** greatest of Spanish churches, finished 1506) begun. The chief architects were perhaps German.

1402-3   Renewed conspiracies in England, allied with Glendower and Douglas, and headed by Harry Percy (Hotspur), the Earl of Northumberland (Hotspur's father), Scrope, Archbishop of York, and others. This conspiracy crushed at the battle of Shrewsbury (July 1403).

1402-6   French adventurers' conquest of the Northern Canaries. Beginnings of a permanent European rule and settlement in the Atlantic Islands.

1402-5   Spanish embassy (headed by Ruy Goncalvez de Clavijo) to the court of Timur. With this ends European official intercourse with Inner Asia for a long time.

1405   **Death of Timur,** at Otrar in Western Central Asia, on his way to attack China. **Dissolution of the Second Mongol Empire.** The gradual disappearance of the Mongol states follows. (But in the sixteenth century, from 1526, a descendant of Timur founds a Third Mongol Empire in India, the dominion of ' the Great Mogul '.) The conversion of most of the Western Mongols to Islam is completed during Timur's lifetime. Ruin of Christian hopes. The Eastern Mongols mainly won to Buddhism.

1406-10   The Parliaments of these years appear to mark the **zenith of mediaeval constitutional life in England.** (Elections to Parliament safeguarded ; an audit of the grants from the Commons to the Crown secured ; the Commons' sole right to originate money grants conceded ; perfect freedom of deliberation between the Houses on money grants recognized ; proposals to confiscate Church property for military purposes, &c.)

1407, &c.   Increasing civil strife in France (' Burgundians ' and ' Armagnacs ' (1410)). Murder of the Duke of Orleans by order of the Duke of Burgundy. The English Government first helps the Burgundians (1411), then the Orleanists or Armagnacs (1412).

The *Council of Pisa* tries to end the Great Schism, but **1409** fails, only adding a third line of rival popes.

Hussite troubles in Prague. Violent quarrels between **1409** Germans and Chekhs, the latter inclining to Wycliffism. All German professors and students leave the University and migrate to Leipzig.

Foundation of the University of Leipzig, the earliest **1409** in Germany proper, largely by migration from Prague. University library at Leipzig established.

Death of Froissart.   **1410**

Election of Sigismund or Siegmund, King of Hungary, **1410** brother of Wenceslaus (Wenzel), as emperor.

Defeat of the Teutonic Knights at **Tannenberg** or Grün- **1410** wald by the united Poles and Lithuanians [see 1386]. This event, largely the result of the conversion of Lithuania and its union with Poland, marks the commencement of a long ebb of Germanic influence and aggression in the Baltic lands, and of a remarkable Slavonic revival, first under Poland, then under Russia. This process of German decline is not arrested till the rise of Brandenburg-Prussia under the Great Elector (especially from about 1657).

Papal buildings in extension of the Vatican Palace, **1410–17** Rome.

Foundation of the University of St. Andrews, the earliest **1411** in Scotland.

Re-foundation of the University of Pavia (see 1110 (?), **1412** 1361), which, in the fifteenth century, enjoys its most brilliant success.

Accession of Henry V ('the great Lancastrian') in **1413** England. The Lancastrian alliance with the Church strengthened. Incipient, and fruitless, Lollard rising, in connexion with the condemnation of Sir John Oldcastle (Lord Cobham).

1414   The **Council of Constance** (1414–18) summoned by Pope John XXIII and the Emperor Sigismund (at Constance on the Lake of Constance).

Pope John, whose deposition by any real Council of the Church was probable enough, struggles against pressure from all sides—the Emperor leading—but is forced to consent.

This Council is (a) the most important assembly of the Church since the Lateran Council of 1215, or in many respects throughout the whole of the Middle Ages proper (since the fifth century).

(b) A Diet or Council of the Empire.

(c) A European Congress.

It is perhaps the most representative gathering of *Latin* Christendom, as a whole, at any time. ' The number of ecclesiastics present, with their attendants, is reckoned at 18,000. During the . . . Council there were usually 50,000 strangers within the walls of Constance : sometimes twice that number. . . . Among those attracted . . . by hope of gain were . . . merchants, lawyers in great numbers and in all varieties, artists and craftsmen, players, jugglers, and musicians ' (Robertson).

The Council is opened November 5, 1414, by Pope John XXIII ; the first general session is held November 16 ; full business begins with the arrival of Sigismund, December 25. The leading spirit of the Council at first is John Gerson, Chancellor of the University of Paris, who does most to procure the condemnation of Hus and Jerome, but is defeated in his efforts for Church reform.

Three main objects of the Council :

(a) *Causa Unionis*, or the unity of the Church and the suppression of the schism.

(b) *Causa Reformationis*, or the reform of the Church ' in head and members '—by this is meant the ending of practical abuses, not the alteration of doctrine.

(c) *Causa Fidei*, or the reassertion of the faith and the suppression of heresy.

Meeting of disaffected Lollards at St. Giles's Fields, **1414** London, dispersed. Fresh English statute against Lollard opinions.

Parliamentary control of legislation in England strength- **1414** ened (enactment that statutes shall be promulgated without alteration of the petitions on which they are based).

Parliament confiscates the ' alien priories ' in England (property of religious houses belonging to foreigners) and grants them to the Crown. Note the strengthening of national and royal control over the Church in England— another forecast of the sixteenth-century Reformation.

The Council of Constance decides its method of voting **1415** (by ' nations '), settles all preliminaries, and proceeds to business (February).

Four ' nations ' are recognized at first—Italian, German, French, English, to which the Spanish is added later. The method of formation is highly arbitrary—thus the English ' nation ' is made to include Ireland, Arabia, Media, Persia, India, Ethiopia, Egypt, Marocco, and the ' land of Prester John '.

PERIOD XXVII

**FROM THE COUNCIL OF CONSTANCE, THE REOPEN-
ING OF THE HUNDRED YEARS' WAR, AND THE
BEGINNING OF THE PORTUGUESE EXPANSION, TO
THE CAPTURE OF CONSTANTINOPLE BY THE OTTO-
MAN TURKS, AND THE BEGINNING OF THE GREAT
AGE OF THE CLASSICAL RENAISSANCE IN WESTERN
EUROPE, 1415–53**

GENERAL POINTS

1. The **Council of Constance ends the schism, condemns
Wycliffe and Hus, but fails** to effect a thorough **reform**
of the Church. Later efforts to maintain the **conciliar
movement of reform frustrated.**

2. Last period of the **Hundred Years' War, which ends
with the expulsion of the English from** all **France** [except
Calais] and the destruction of their continental empire,
inherited from William the Conqueror and Henry II.

3. **Revival of the French monarchy and nation,** after
terrible sufferings. Tendency towards strong centralized
government ('New Monarchy') here and all over Europe.

4. Practical **collapse of the constitutional régime** in
England. Beginnings of *civil strife* ('Wars of Roses').

5. Progress of **Portuguese expansion.** Discoveries in
the Atlantic and along the west coast of Africa. The
Equator approached.

6. **Fall of Constantinople and end of the Eastern Empire.**
Ottoman Turkish dominion in its place. Flight of Byzantines to W. Europe.

7. Gradual *weakening of Mongol Tartar power in Russia.* Moscow tends to become fully independent, and to carry with it great part of the Russian land.

8. The '*Hussite Wars*', ending in a compromise, by which the Church has to some extent to admit defeat (forecast of sixteenth-century disasters). Military importance of Hussite struggle. New methods of warfare.

9. Beginnings of the *Hohenzollerns in Brandenburg.*

10. Progress of **European civilization.** The great age of the **Classical Renaissance** begins, especially in Italy. Mediaeval conditions and the mediaeval spirit are now rapidly passing away. Interest in the **New Learning. Invention of printing.** Reintroduction and cheapening of **paper.** Growth of libraries. New universities.

Literature, science, and art. Marvellous **artistic developments.** Effect of **geographical and scientific discoveries.** Development of **firearms,** changing the whole of war. 'At the threshold of the modern world.'

1415   **Henry V of England claims the French crown,** summons the Great Council [Magnum Concilium], and declares war with their assent.

1415   Proceedings of the **Council of Constance,** which **asserts** the **supremacy of** a General **Council,** properly summoned, **over** any **Pope.**

The three Popes of the schism removed :

(a) Pope John XXIII compelled to abdicate (May 29).

(b) Resignation of Pope Gregory XII (July 4).

(c) Benedict XIII deserted by his supporters (December). ' The harmless old man was left in a solitary castle to excommunicate twice each day the rebel kingdoms which had deserted his cause ' [Gibbon].

The **Great Schism** is now practically **ended,** and all is now clear for the election of a fresh Pope for all Latin Christendom.

John **Hus** summoned before the Council, imprisoned, **condemned, and executed** as a leader of heresy (July 6).

Hus's friend, Jerome of Prague, arrested and imprisoned (finally condemned and executed, 1416).

The Emperor Sigismund grants the Mark of Brandenburg to his stanch supporter, Frederick of Hohenzollern, Burggrave of Nuremberg. *Beginning of the Hohenzollern dynasty in Brandenburg* (and later Prussia).

Outbreak of hostilities between England and France. Henry V lands at Le Havre, captures Harfleur (September), and defeats a French army at *Agincourt* (Azincourt), (October 25).

1415   Capture of Ceuta in Africa (opposite Gibraltar) by the Portuguese (August 24). Beginning of the Portuguese Empire in Morocco, and of the great **Portuguese age of expansion** generally.

Prince **Henry of Portugal,** ' the Navigator ', third son of King John, sends out his first expeditions into the Atlantic or along W. Africa.

Portuguese ships arrive at the island of Grand Canary **1415** [already well known to explorers] and take possession of part of it.

Visit of the Emperor Sigismund to France and England. **1416** His fruitless efforts to reconcile the combatants and unite them in a league against the Turks : he is more successful in winning general approval for the measures of the Council, already taken, or in contemplation, for healing the schism, for reform, and for the faith—[*Causa Unionis, Causa Reformationis, Causa Fidei* : see 1414].

The Portuguese pass beyond Cape Bojador, hitherto the (usual) limit of exploring knowledge in West Africa, slightly south of Morocco.

English alliance with Burgundy against France.

Proceedings at Constance. Long discussions on Church reform, mainly ineffective.

Execution of Jerome of Prague.

Paving of London streets begun (?).   **1417**

Frederick of Hohenzollern formally invested with the Mark of Brandenburg [see 1415].

Election of Cardinal Otto Colonna as *Pope Martin V* (November 11). The last age of the mediaeval Papacy begins with him.

Henry V of England begins the systematic conquest of **1417** Normandy.

Martin V *dissolves the Council of Constance* (April 1418), **1418** having *evaded all real measures of Church reform.* He returns to Rome in May 1418. He does much to restore the prosperity and stateliness of the city, and is called by flatterers ' the third founder of Rome '.

Outbreak of the '**Hussite Wars**' in Bohemia (1419– **1419** 36), ' the first great military struggle of Protestantism '. Burning indignation of Hus's followers at the treatment of their leader.

Hussite demands for the concession of the chalice to the laity—hence the name *Calixtines* [otherwise for *Communion in both kinds*, ' sub utraque specie '—hence the name *Utraquists*]—for *free preaching*, *&c.*

Terrible results of the war, waged with the utmost ferocity on both sides. Wholesale destruction of ancient buildings and monuments in Bohemia and neighbouring lands.

John Ziska and Prokop, the chief Hussite leaders (commanders of genius), win many victories.

Use of gunpowder, great clumsy cannon, and *wagonlagers* by the Hussites.

1418–20   Portuguese discovery and exploration of the Madeiras (already imperfectly known ; see 1351).

Progress of the war in France. English capture of Rouen and conquest of Normandy.

1418–20   Massacre of ' Orleanists ' in Paris (1418). Assassination of John [Jean ' sans Peur '], Duke of Burgundy, at Montereau, by the ' Armagnacs ' or party of the Dauphin (1419). Philip the Good, John's successor, allies with the English (Treaty of Troyes, 1420).

1419   Foundation of the University of Rostock, in N. Germany.

1420   *Treaty of Troyes* (May 21). Henry V, recognized as regent and heir of France, marries Catherine, daughter of Charles VI. On the death of Charles VI the two crowns are to be for ever united in the person of Henry V and his successors. English and Burgundians masters of Paris.

1421–2   Brilliant successes of the Bohemian Hussites, led by Ziska, against Roman Catholic crusaders. Sigismund— now (from 1419) King of Bohemia, as well as Emperor— himself defeated.

1421   The banker Giovanni (John) de' *Medici* acquires

supreme power *in Florence*, and practically subverts the
republic, founding the rule of his family in its place.

Death of Henry V of England. Accession of the infant **1422**
Henry VI.
Death of Charles VI of France. His son, Charles VII,
succeeds to the leadership of the national cause in France.

The Ottoman Turks, who have gradually restored their **1422**
power after Timur's attack, besiege Constantinople afresh.

Continued successes of the English in France, under **1422–9**
the leadership of the Duke of Bedford.

Beginning of the University Library at Cambridge.   **1425**
Prince Henry, ' the Navigator ', of Portugal, begins the
settlement of the Madeiras—the beginning of Portuguese
colonization. This is one of the best starting-points for
' modern colonial history '.

Foundation of the University of Louvain, the ' Belgian **1426**
Athens '.

Progress of the English advance in France.   **1428–9**
Siege of Orleans.

The war in France changed by the appearance of **Jeanne 1429**
Darc (' Joan of Arc ', ' La Pucelle ', a peasant girl of
Domrémy in Eastern Champagne, on the Meuse, roused
by patriotism and religious fervour to save her country).
She relieves Orleans (April), defeats the English, and
brings Charles VII in triumph to Rheims, where he is
crowned (July).

Death of John Gerson (b. 1363), ' Doctor Chris- **1429**
tianissimus ', ' Doctor Consolatorius ', the leading spirit
in the Councils of Pisa and Constance, Chancellor of Paris
University, 1395–1417 (?). In theology a mystic. The
later scholasticism repelled him. He was anxious to revive
the study of the Bible and the Fathers in place of ' unprofit-
able questions of the Schools '. He is above all famous

as the great advocate of conservative Church reform, through General Councils, who were to be supreme even over popes [see 1414–15]. He was bitterly hostile to the early Protestantism, and the condemnation and execution of Hus was largely due to him.

1430   Signs of anti-democratic reaction in England (restriction of county franchise to forty-shilling freeholders).

1430   City Library of Ratisbon [Regensburg] founded—the oldest existing town-library of Germany.

1430   The Andrea Bianco map of this year indicates the Sargasso Sea or Sea of Seaweed, S. of the Azores, in mid-Atlantic [see 1448].

1431   Jeanne Darc, having fallen into the power of the English, is burned as a witch at Rouen.

1431   Foundation of the University of Poitiers.

1431–49   *Council of Basel*, the last of the reforming councils of the fifteenth century, and the only result of the Constance decree ordering regular and frequent councils.   In the main it is a failure, and shows the collapse of the reforming movement.   Almost its only achievement is the compromise with the Hussites [see 1433].

1431–9   Portuguese re-discovery and earliest colonization of the *Azores* or ' Hawk Islands '—sighted by Europeans, probably Genoese, in the fourteenth century, but hitherto uninhabited and but slightly known.   This group is fully one-third of the way to America [Lisbon—Florida].

1433   The Council of Basel concludes an *agreement* (the Prague *Compactata*) *with* the moderate *Hussites*, granting their chief demands—the cup to the laity in the Communion ; free preaching ; exemption from Ecclesiastical Courts.

The extreme Hussites reject the *compact* and are cut to pieces (1433–6).

About this time, highest importance of the Secret **1430–60** Tribunals (*Vehmgerichte, Femgerichte*) in Germany.

Death of the Duke of Bedford.   **1435**

The Duke of Burgundy breaks off the English alliance **1435** and joins France. (Death-blow to English hopes of French conquest.)

Growth of the power of Burgundy at the expense both of France and the Empire, favoured, since 1415—

(*a*) By the English attack upon France.

(*b*) By the Hussite troubles and German disasters.

The Portuguese begin again [see 1415–16] a vigorous **1434–6** advance to the south (along West Africa) beyond the farthest known. Coasting of the Sahara begun.

The French recover Paris, and gradually win great part **1436** of the north of France (much of Normandy, &c.). End of the Hussite Wars.

Foundation of the University of Caen, Normandy, under **1437** English auspices (re-founded under French auspices, 1452).

Foundation of All Souls College, Oxford (library, 1443). **1437**

About this time the English Privy Council again loses **1437–40** connexion with Parliament, and is nominated entirely by the Crown (another indication of anti-democratic reaction).

Edinburgh finally becomes the capital of Scotland, displac- **c. 1437** ing Perth, &c.

Portuguese failure to conquer Tangier.   **1437**

The *House of Hapsburg* again comes to the *Imperial* **1438** *throne* in Germany, and retains it from this time till the extinction of the *Holy Roman Empire* (1806) [or at least till 1740, and the death of Charles VI, the last direct Hapsburg, after which, through Maria Theresa, the Hapsburg-Lorraine House succeeds].

Beginning of modern standing armies with the Ordinance **1439**

of Orleans (institution of regular companies, and abolition of the ' free companies ') in France.

1440   King's College, Cambridge, founded by Henry VI [the chapel, the ' glory of Cambridge ', one of the finest Gothic choirs in the world, is begun six years later].

1441-2   Progress of the Portuguese discoveries along West Africa. The **first slaves and gold dust** brought home from the Sahara coast (Northern *Guinea*). Beginnings of the modern slave-trade.

1443   *Copenhagen becomes* the royal residence of the Danish kings and the *capital of Denmark.*

1444   *Crusade against the Ottoman Turks,* led by ' Ladislaus ' [Wladislaw], King of Hungary and Poland, and John Huniades, the Hungarian hero, *utterly defeated at Varna,* on the Black Sea, by Murad [' Amurath '] II. This is the *last serious attempt to save Christian Constantinople,* which is now left to its fate. The migration of Byzantines, especially scholars and men of letters, to Western Europe becomes more and more notable, and greatly helps the Classical Renaissance, especially in Italy.

' Ladislaus ' having perished at Varna [' Hungarians, behold the head of your king '], Huniades is appointed Regent of Hungary (1444–52).

1444   Beginnings of the *University Library of Oxford,* through the gifts of Duke Humphrey of Gloucester (refounded by Sir Thomas Bodley in 1602, and since known as the ' Bodleian ').

1444-5   The *Portuguese,* coasting West Africa, pass beyond the Sahara shore, and *reach* the Senegal and *the real negro land,* south of the desert. They *round Cape Verde,* the westernmost point of Africa.

Progress of their exploration and colonization in the Azores and Madeiras.

They also *begin the exploration of the Sahara interior.*

Prince Henry fails in his repeated efforts to secure the Canaries for Portugal, through the opposition of Castile.

Death of Brunelleschi, the architect (builder of the dome **1444** of Florence Cathedral).

The Portuguese reach the neighbourhood of Sierra **1445–6** Leone, and begin to advance eastwards (towards the Indies, as they hope).

Chapel of King's College, Cambridge, commenced [see **1446** 1440], finished 1515.

Town Hall of Louvain commenced (finished 1463).   **1447**

Pontificate of Nicolas V. Bloom of the **Classical Renais- 1447–55 sance in Italy.**

The Portuguese further organize their African slave- **c. 1448** trade and build their first fort, factory, and mission station at Arguin Island in Northern *Guinea*, near Cape Blanco.

The *Andrea Bianco* map of 1448 contains delineation of land WSW. of Cape Verde, which has been [wrongly] conjectured to indicate a discovery of S. America about this time [see 1430]. It is probably an imaginary island.

The war in France, after thirteen to fourteen years of **1449** inaction or practical truce, is vigorously renewed by the French, who reconquer most of Normandy.

About this time, beginning of Hurstmonceaux Castle, **c. 1450** a typical example of the transition from castle to mansion in W. Europe.

Rebellion of Jack Cade—a fresh *Jacquerie* or peasant **1450** insurrection—in England (partly a result of the French disasters).

The Town Hall of Brussels practically completed (begun **1450** 1402).

Nicolas V *begins* (*the present*) *St. Peter's, Rome.* But **1450** work is now only begun. The main part of the church is of the next century. Nicolas V plans also a vast extension of the *Vatican Palace*, and is the refounder of the *Vatican Library* in its present form. The Papal library can be traced back, however, at least to the middle of the fifth century [see c. 450] ; it was at the Lateran Palace till the Avignon captivity (1309–78), and only after the return from Avignon is fixed at the Vatican.

c. 1450   **Invention of Modern Printing** (i. e. printing by movable types, &c.) at Mainz by John Gutenberg (Gensfleisch) and others.

1450   A Catalan map of this year suggests a great southern projection for Africa, as in the Laurentian Portolano of 1351,—and in fact.

1451   Accession of Sultan Mahomet II, the captor of Constantinople.

1452   Last coronation of an emperor at Rome [Frederick III, sometimes reckoned as Frederick IV].

1440–53   Fresh beginnings of the Royal Library of France [now *Bibliothèque Nationale*] under Charles VII. The old Bibliothèque Royale had been carried to England by the Duke of Bedford and dispersed.

1453   **End of the Hundred Years' War** between France and England, with the complete defeat of the English, and their final expulsion from all their possessions in France (except Calais and the small territory adjacent). Talbot, Earl of Shrewsbury, is defeated and killed at the battle of Castillon (on the frontier of Guienne and Périgord). Surrender of Bordeaux and all the south-west ; the rest of France had been already recovered by the French monarchy.

The greatness of France begins afresh, to be interrupted by the Italian Wars and the Religious Civil Wars [1494–1598].

In England the disastrous close of the Hundred Years' War is largely responsible for the *Wars of the Roses*, and the *discrediting of* the old *Parliamentary Liberalism*, especially in its more recent and advanced forms—'the Lancastrian experiment'. Thus it leads to the *New Monarchy* of Edward IV, Richard III, and the Tudors.

Final siege and **capture of Constantinople by the Ottoman 1453 Turks** under Mahomet II. ['One God in Heaven, and one Lord on earth, and I am that Lord.']

Flight of Byzantine (Greek-speaking) scholars, &c., to W. Europe.

Beginning of the **great age of the Classical Renaissance** in Italy (to a less extent in Germany, France, and England, &c.).

The fall of Constantinople is among the foremost of the events that mark the end of the Middle Ages, just as the foundation of the city is one of the events that mark the passing of the Ancient Civilization.

GENERAL VIEW OF THE STATE OF EUROPE AT THE CLOSE OF THE MIDDLE AGES, ABOUT 1453

Once more, remarkable changes are visible [see *General View . . . about* 1303].

Mediaeval Civilization has begun to pass into Modern. The power of the Church, though still immense, is now weakened. On the surface, its splendour and prosperity are little impaired—not so its real hold upon the races and the thought of Christendom. Those aspects, or products, of Mediaeval Civilization specially favoured by the Church—e. g. the Monastic System, the Scholastic Philosophy, the Orders of Chivalry—have lost ground, and are passing out of fashion. Ideas and tendencies rootedly hostile to the Mediaeval Church have developed—especially that love and imitation of pre-Christian Classical Antiquity which inspire the Classical Renaissance. Largely through the assistance of this spirit, Free Thought has also revived.

A disposition towards unbounded inquiry and criticism is developed in the fifteenth century, more than at any earlier time in human history. Mediaeval forgeries and blunders begin to be exposed. Mediaeval assumptions are everywhere challenged. Men begin to treat the Schoolmen and their system with contempt. The last phase of Scholasticism passes into Mysticism. Monasticism becomes unpopular : monasteries decay for want of support. An early type of definite Protestantism has appeared (e. g. in Wycliffe and Hus)—identical in all essential respects with one or other of the leading Protestant schools of the sixteenth century. Despite fierce struggles, this early Protestantism survives in certain quarters. In some quarters a neo-Paganism begins to be cultivated. Neo-Classicism is dominant in Literature and Art.

The New Literatures of the West have made much progress since the opening of the fourteenth century. Dante, Boccaccio, Chaucer, and others have shown what the New Languages can do.

The growth of Classicism, though in certain respects very injurious, is unable to stop the growth of these New Languages and Literatures. In some ways it even stimulates the latter remarkably.

The interest in Nature has strengthened and deepened. Natural Science, by the middle of the fifteenth century, is really far more advanced than at any earlier period in history—the ' scientific spirit ' far more awakened and energetic.

The widespread use of the mariner's compass, the discovery of gunpowder, the development of firearms, the invention of printing, the improvement in the manufacture of paper, are among the chief results of this advance, which powerfully aids the Classical Renaissance, the new Free Thought, and to a large extent even the Protestant Reformation (suspicious and often hostile as the latter is at heart towards the scientific spirit).

The arts of Painting and Sculpture, especially the former, are awakened to new life by the Classical Revival. The masterpieces of antiquity are rivalled, approached, or surpassed. The ' supreme pictorial age ' begins. Architecture in Northern Europe passes into the latest and most sumptuous varieties of ' Gothic ' or ' Pointed ' : everything suggests the coming abandonment of this style and the coming imitation of Classical models. In Southern European buildings the Classical Revival is already winning the day.

The economic development of Christendom (since 1300) has been unequal. On the whole, the wealth and material civilization of Europe have advanced. But most of the Commercial Republics and Free Cities of Italy have now (by 1450) seen their best days. Many of them have already

P

fallen under the rule of despots. Far greater commercial prosperity and vitality are to be seen in Northern Europe, especially in Flanders.

Over much of Europe—e.g. in France, England, Italy, Spain, Portugal, Russia, the Balkan Peninsula—the free life of earlier time is now cut short. The end of the Middle Ages, the beginning of Modern History, is an era of ' New Monarchy '. Strong centralized governments more and more rule the organized nationalities, which have taken or are taking shape. Allied or related peoples coalesce under one dynasty—as in the cases of Poland-Lithuania, Denmark-Sweden-Norway, or various Russian principalities under Moscow [Castile-Aragon union comes but a few years later ; that of England and Scotland, after another century and a half of conflict and approximation].

The European overland expansion has ended in ruin—mainly through the break-up of the Mongol Empire, the conversion of the Western Tartars to Islam, and the fresh progress of the Muhammadan Turks under new leaders, the Ottomans.

But the overland movement is replaced by that oversea. Beginning while the former is in full vigour, the latter only acquires decisive importance in the fifteenth century, under Portuguese leadership, after the collapse of the overland experiment. By 1450 considerable progress has been made in the exploration of the Atlantic, and in the discovery of the ocean route round Africa to Asia. Canaries, Madeiras, Azores, have been colonized ; Sierra Leone has been reached ; the Equator closely approached. Everything is prepared for the revelations of the next age—the Cape of Good Hope, the Indian Ocean, America.

In the separate states of Christendom the effects of these changes are no less clear :

The **PAPACY,** degraded by the Avignon captivity and the long subservience to France, is further injured and

humiliated by the Great Schism which immediately follows
the return from Avignon. It is also weakened by the
outbreak of powerful anti-Church religious movements,
especially in England and Bohemia. The Conciliar Movement of Reform threatens to subjugate it to a permanent
series of representative Church Assemblies. Delivered from
the schism by the Council of Constance, the Papacy, by
skilful diplomacy, gets the better of the Council, makes
truce with Bohemian Protestantism, and is apparently
victorious over English Wycliffism. But this victory is
never complete. At the end of the Middle Ages the Papacy
becomes intimately allied with the Classical Revival, an
alliance which produces unexpected and disastrous results
in the semi-paganizing of the Roman see and court.
Here is a main cause of the great Protestant revolt of
the sixteenth century, and, in its turn, of the Catholic
revival.

The **EASTERN EMPIRE,** after a long and slow decay
[1204–1453], has become the prey of the Ottoman Turks.
The fall of Constantinople produces vital effects on culture,
as on politics.

The **WESTERN EMPIRE,** now permanently associated
with the House of Hapsburg, Vienna, and the Duchy of
Austria, has now lost its hold almost altogether on Burgundy and the other imperial possessions of the Burgundian
House (e. g. in the Netherlands). Its hold over Italy is
now (1450) a distant memory. In **GERMANY** itself the
imperial unity has really disappeared. The German kingdom tends steadily towards a loose agglomeration of
practically independent states, under the permanent but
ineffective headship of Austria. In the separate states
the local rulers gradually become all-powerful. Though
many of the cities are still remarkably rich and prosperous,
political feudalism is generally and fatally in the ascendant.
The expansion of the Germanic race is checked [in the

fifteenth century] by Slavonic revival : the Teutonic Order, like the Hanseatic League, is now declining.

Among the other European states—

FRANCE has been checked for more than a century by the Hundred Years' War [1338–1453]. At the opening of this struggle she already seemed the first power in Western Christendom : at the end she is about to be rivalled, and for a time surpassed, by the new Spain [the Castile-Aragon monarchy]. Though terribly exhausted by the war with England, she has finally got the better of her old enemy, on her own soil. From all the old French land, practically, the English have been expelled. In Southern Burgundy the French kingdom has made important advances beyond old limits. In Northern Burgundy and the north-east she is still threatened [like the Empire] with the growth of the new 'Middle State' of the Dukes of Burgundy. (This menace proves only temporary.) Internally, the French crown has for the time lost some of its power. The noblesse emerges with new strength from the Hundred Years' War. A fresh struggle is needed for the complete and final victory of the royal power.

ENGLAND, after brilliant successes, has been finally defeated in her attempts at continental empire. The shock of the French disasters is a chief cause of the breakdown, or suspension, of her constitutional developments, and even, for a brief interval, of so much of her political order and stability. Something of the anarchy of Stephen's time seems, on the surface, to return in the Wars of the Roses. The Middle Ages [by 1453] leave England apparently more weakened and depressed than at any time since Edward II. Yet her continental victories [Crécy, &c.], politically fruitless, are of high moral value. The final failure of the fifteenth century in France helps to turn her towards the true path of her development—maritime power, oversea development, world-wide trade, colonial

empire. The national wealth and material prosperity
steadily increase throughout the fourteenth and fifteenth
centuries.

In **ITALY** most of the Commercial Republics and Free
Cities have fallen under despots or foreign rulers. Yet the
' tyranny ' of the Medici in Florence brings the city to the
zenith of its material prosperity, culture, and power :
the rule of Aragon in Naples and Sicily is welcomed after
the brief interval of French rule : Milan is never more
important, politically, than under the Visconti and Sforza.
Even Venice, which retains her republican constitution,
becomes a far stricter oligarchy : she also is at her ' noon-
day ' in the fifteenth century.

Every Italian state, almost, is now [*c.* 1450] pervaded
by the Classical Revival, with its worship of ancient
models in literature, art, and manners ; its ' endeavour to
reconstitute man as a free being ', not as the servant of
a theological system ; its passionate appreciation of the
present life and the visible world. The darker side of al
this becomes clearer in the next age.

In **SPAIN** there has been no great political change
since the opening of the fourteenth century, except for the
decisive assertion of Portuguese independence under the
House of Aviz. The maritime and colonial expansion of
Portugal in the Atlantic and along West Africa under
Prince Henry the Navigator, and the growth of Aragon
as a Mediterranean power, especially in Italy, belong
rather to general history. The formation of the great
Spanish monarchy by the union of Castile and Aragon
belongs to the next generation and the next two decades.
The old free institutions are now [*c.* 1450] rapidly and
permanently declining in all the Spanish states.

The **SCANDINAVIAN STATES** have been united by
the Union of Kalmar, but Sweden is already showing
signs of restlessness, foreshadowing the rupture of the

Union in the next century. Thus a unique political opportunity is lost. But at the close of the Middle Ages [c. 1453]
the joint monarchy, under the Danish kings, is one of the
European 'Great Powers'. Even here the tendency towards
' New Monarchy ' is traceable.

HUNGARY is at the height of its power and prosperity
throughout the latest Middle Ages, and acts as the true
leader of all effective European resistance to the Ottoman
Turks at this time. Hungarian sovereignty, or supremacy,
is repeatedly asserted over various neighbouring states :
the Hungarian kingdom is a dangerous menace to Venice.
No one in 1453 could have readily foreseen the ruin of
Hungary in the next century.

POLAND, united with **LITHUANIA** since the end of
the fourteenth century, victorious over the Teutonic
Knights at the beginning of the fifteenth, aggrandized by
vast acquisitions from Western Russia, has become [c.
1450] in area of territory perhaps the largest of Christian
states, and seemingly one of the strongest and most
influential. But, socially and constitutionally, the internal
weakness of Poland is in contrast to her apparent political
and military power. The Polish ' Republic ', hampered
by the elective kingship and by an omnipotent parliament
or diet of notables, tends more and more to feudalization,
to the destruction of the central power by the nobles and
gentry, and to the degradation and oppression of the
lower classes by the landowners, great and small.

The **RUSSIAN STATES,** so long the prey of Tartars,
Lithuanians, Poles, and others, since the Mongol conquest
in the thirteenth century, have begun in the fourteenth
to find a new national centre in Moscow. Slowly but
steadily their history in the fifteenth has moved towards
independence and recovery in the East. But the Tartar
suzerainty has not yet been thrown off [by 1453], although
this event will be one of the features of the next genera-

tion [1480]. Russia, except the western half conquered by Poland-Lithuania, will be reunited under Moscow [1471] before emancipation from the Mongol is fully achieved. Taught by the lessons of the past, the Moscow princes evolve, and the Russian people submit to, a centralized autocratic monarchy of the strictest type. This at least ensures safety from the democratic and oligarchic disorders and schisms which had ruined the old free Russia.

Lastly, in the South-East, the Ottoman **TURKS** have already [by 1453] established a Muhammadan despotic empire in Europe—as in Asia—as extensive as the Byzantine in the days of its power. In the next century [1450–1570] this dominion is destined to vast extension : it seems for a moment to threaten Christendom, like the early Saracens. Yet its power, under the ablest Sultans, is greater in appearance than in reality ; its administration and organization, except for war, are so defective that its military successes are often hampered or nullified. But as a fighting state it is, for the time, very formidable ; not till the end of the seventeenth century is it clearly unable to cope with the best Christian armies, even for defence.

In the Far East of Europe and in Upper Asia the **TARTAR** empires have passed away, leaving only fragments which will soon pass under the rule of new and restored states and races. Thus Moscovite Russia will soon [after 1453] repudiate the overlordship of the *Golden Horde*, and then subjugate the khanates into which the Horde is broken.

Looking back to the opening of the eleventh century [c. 1000] or to the fall of the old Roman Empire in the West [c. 410–76], the decisive progress of the chief European races is clear enough in almost every field of civilization. The new nations, enjoying a life on the whole so much more healthy, free, and progressive than that of the

Roman world, have through many trials grown to manhood. And they are now [c. 1450] at the beginning of unlimited development. The barriers of ancient knowledge have been broken through in every direction. Europeans have begun to traverse the oceans and continents beyond their own homes, taking with them their race and politics and culture, and preparing for the European domination of the entire world. New inventions have made or are making a revolution in natural science, and giving man— European man—a control over nature unknown before. This advance will in time produce fundamental changes in the conditions and possibilities of life. A second-rate European power of recent centuries, especially of the last two or three generations, overmatches in military strength the whole empire of the Caesars. The conveniences, appliances, and luxuries of the most modern era would be difficult of belief to past ages. Nowhere is this more apparent than in economic development. How can the commerce of the classical or the mediaeval civilization, at its most prosperous epochs, be compared with that of the present ? Before the end of the Middle Ages Europeans of the Christian civilization had already expressed them-selves in the new literatures and in art with as much wisdom, taste, and genius as in the best ages of Hellas, India, or Rome. And here, as elsewhere, mediaeval develop-ment is followed, and in many ways surpassed, by 'modern times '—with all their faults and evils, the ' crown of history '.

ADDITIONAL NOTE TO 1164 [p. 123]

By the Constitutions of Clarendon, clause 3 : ' A Clerk accused of any matter, when summoned by the king's justiciar, shall come into his court, and there answer for what it shall seem good to the king's court that he should answer for there, and in the Church court for what it shall seem good that he should answer for there : so that the king's justiciar shall send into the Church court to see how the case is there tried, and if the clerk shall be convicted, the Church ought not to defend him further.'

INDEX

Eric the Red, 80, 84.
Erigena, John Scotus, 68.
Eusebius, 5.

Fatimites, 90.
Ferdinand III of Castile, St., 140–3.
France,French, see *Verdun,Franks, Charles the Bald, Louis VI, VII, IX, Philip Augustus, Philip the Fair, Suger,* &c.
Francis of Assisi, St., 134, 136.
Franciscan Order, 134, 136, 147, 156, 175–6.
Franks, Frankish race, Frankish Empire, 11–12, 19, 22, 23–4, 32, 35–6, 39, 42–3, 47–9, 50–6 ; see *Holy Roman Empire.*
Frederick of Swabia, Frederick I (Barbarossa), Emperor, 118–19.
Frederick II, Emperor, 135, 139–41.
Frederick III, Emperor, 206.
Frederick III of Hohenzollern, 153.
Frederick VI of Hohenzollern, 198.

Genoa, 153–4, 156, 175, 177, 187.
Genseric (Gaiseric), 16.
Gepids, 35.
Gerald de Barri, 139.
Gerbert, Sylvester II, 84.
Gerson, John, 194, 201–2.
Germany, Germans, see *Goths, Franks, Burgundians, Saxons,* &c. ; *Alaric, Theodoric, Clovis,* &c.; *Charles the Great,* &c. ; *Henry the Fowler ; Otto I, II, III ; Henry II, III, IV, V, VI, VII ; Frederick I, II ; Conrad II, III,* &c.
Giotto, 158.
Giraldus Cambrensis, see *Gerald de Barri.*
Glaber, Ralph, 93.
Glendower, see *Owen Glendower.*
Gnesen, 74, 170–1
Godfrey of Bouillon, 111.
Goths, Gothic race, 11–12, 14–16, 28–9, 48.
Gower, 189.
Gregory I ('the Great'), Pope, 37–8.

Gregory II, 64.
Gregory VI, 95.
Gregory VII, Hildebrand, 94–5, 101, 103, 104, 106, 107, 124.
Gregory X, 152.
Gregory XI, 183.
Gutenberg, John, 206.

Hadrian I, 54.
Hadrian IV, 122.
Hakim Biamrillah, 89.
Hansa, Hanseatic League, 147, 151, 178–80, 181–2.
Harald Fairhair, 64–5.
Harald Hardrada, 98, 100.
Harold, son of Godwine, 97, 100.
Harun-ar-Rashid, 55.
Hedwig, 188.
Helena, 2.
Henry I of Germany ('the Fowler'), 74–5.
Henry II of Germany, Emperor, 91.
Henry III of Germany, Emperor, 93–5, 97–8.
Henry IV of Germany, Emperor, 98, 101–3, 112.
Henry V of Germany, Emperor, 112–13.
Henry VI of Germany, Emperor, 129–30.
Henry VII of Germany, Emperor, 168–9.
Henry I of England, 111–12.
Henry II of England, 119–20, 123–5.
Henry III of England, 138, 141, 148–9.
Henry IV of England, 190.
Henry V of England, 193, 198–9, 200–1.
Henry VI of England, 201.
Henry the Lion, of Saxony, &c., 124, 125, 129–30.
Henry the Navigator, 213.
Heraclius, 39, 41.
Hermann of Salza, 139.
Hildebrand, see *Gregory VII.*
Hincmar of Rheims, 64.
Hohenzollern House, 153, 198.
Holy Roman Empire, 55–8, 60–1, 68–9, 76, 80, 82, 83–4, 86–7, 91, 92–4, 96–8, 101–4, 112, 113,

Mahmud of Ghazni, 84.
Malachi, Bishop of Armagh, 116.
Manfred, 149.
Maniakes, George, 93.
Manuel Komnenos, 118.
Map, Walter, 130.
Marcel, Etienne, 177.
Marco Polo, see *Polo.*
Margaret of Denmark, Queen, 190.
Margrave, or Elector, of Branden-
burg (Margraviate, Electorate),
178, 198-9 ; see also *Branden-
burg, Hohenzollern.*
Marsilio of Padua, 171, 177.
Martin V, Pope, 199.
Maurice, Emperor, 37.
Medici, John de, 200-1.
Mercia, Mercians, 44-6, 58.
Merovingian or Merwing Dynasty,
House of Clovis, 24, 43, 52.
Methodius, St., 65 ; see *Cyril.*
Mieczyslaw I, 78.
Milan, 122, 124, 188.
Montfort, Simon de, 148-9.
Moscow, 172.
Muawiyah, 46.
Muhammad ('Mahomet'), 34, 39-
41.
Muhammadanism, Islam, 34, 39-
42, &c.
Murad II [' Amurath '], 204.
Musa, 48.

Narses, 28-9.
Neckam, Alexander, 125.
Nestorius, Nestorians, Nestorian-
ism, 21-2, 30, 33.
Nicaea, Council and Creed of, 3,
9 ; Empire of, 133, 148.
Nicolas of Cusa, 191.
Nicolas I, Pope, 63-6.
Nicolas V, Pope, 205-6.
Nikephoros I, 58.
Nikephoros II (Phokas), 58, 75, 78.
Normans, Normandy, 71-2, 93-4,
96-7, 98-106, &c.
Northumbria, Northumbrians,
37-9, 41, 46.
Norway, Norwegians, Northmen,
54-7, 59-60, 62-3, 64-5, 69-71,
72, 80, 82-4, 87-9, 90-2, 93-4,
96-106, &c. : see also *Danes,
Swedes, Harald Fairhair,* &c.

Occam, William of, 176.
Odo (Eudes), 69.
Odovakar (Odoacer), 18.
Olaf, ' the Lap King ', 83.
Olaf Tryggveson, 83-4.
Olaf, St., 90, 92.
Omar, Umar, 44-5.
Orcagna, 183.
Ostrogoths, East Goths, 20-1,
23-4, 28-9.
Oswald, 44-5.
Otto I (' the Great '), 10, 75-9.
Otto II, 80.
Otto III, 80, 83-4.
Otto IV (of Brunswick), 130, 134,
135.
Otto of Bamberg, 115.
Ourique, 117.
Owen Glendower, 191.

Paris, 68, 117-18, 131, 159-60, 177,
182, 194, 206.
Paschal II, Pope, 112.
Patrick, St., 22.
Paul the Deacon, 54.
Payens, Hugh de, see *Hugh de
Payens.*
Penda, 44-6.
Persia, Persians, 30, 34, 36, 37, 38,
39, 41.
Peter of Amiens ('the Hermit'),106.
Peter Lombard, 123.
Petrarch, 167, 182.
Philip II of France ('Augustus'),
128, 130, 133, 134, 140.
Philip IV of France ('the Fair'),
155, 157-60, 167-70.
Philip of Swabia, 134.
Phokas, 37.
Photius, 65.
Piers Plowman, see *Langland.*
Pippin, 51-3.
Poland, Poles, 78, 83, 141, 188,
193 ; see also *Lithuania, Jagel-
lons, Boleslav,* &c.
Polo, Marco, Nicolo, &c., 148, 150,
152-3, 156.
Procopius (Prokopios), Byzantine
historian, 31.
Prokop, Hussite general, 200.

Ravenna, Exarchs of, 29, 52.
Raymond of Lull, see *Lull.*

Recimir, 17.
Richard Cœur de Lion, 128, 129.
Richard II, 183, 187, 190.
Rienzi, 176.
Robert ' Guiscard ', 98, 103, 104.
Robert of Jumièges, 97.
Roger II, 116, 126.
Rolle, Richard, 176.
Roman Empire (incl. *Western* and *Eastern Empires*, but not *Later Western* or *Holy Roman Empire*, which see), *passim* in many sections; see esp. pp. 1, 7–22, 24–33, 42, 44–6, 48–51, 55–6, 58, 66, 75–6, 78–80, 91–2, 93, 96–7, 101, 103, 118, 132–3, 148, 163–4, 178, 180, 189, 191, 201, 204, 206–7, 211.
Rome, *passim* in many sections; see esp. pp. 3, 4, 9, 11, 28–9, 37, 52, 54, 56, 63, 76, 83–4, 94–5, 98, 101, 103–4, 112, 122–4, 130 &c., 136, 158–61, 167, 169, 176, 183, 186, 193, 199, 205–6.
Romulus Augustulus, 17–18.
Rosamund, 36.
Roscelin, 115.
Rubrouck, Rubruquis, 147.
Rupert, Count Palatine, 191.
Rutilius Namatianus, 13.

Saladin, 126, 128.
Salado, see *Tarifa*.
Salamanca, 140, 142.
Salisbury, 148, 177.
Saxons, 12, 16, 53–4, 58, 74 &c., 101, 124–5, 129; see also *English*.
Saxony, 53–4, 58, 74 &c., 101, 124–5, 129.
Scandinavians, 54–60, 62–73, 77, 80, 82–94, 96–8, 104, 144, 190, &c.; see also *Danes, Norwegians, Swedes*.
Schism, the Great, 187, 194, 196, 198.
Scholasticism, Schoolmen, 53, 112, 139, 153–4, 176–7.
Scotland, Scots, 156, 157, 167, 169, 172.
Serbia, Serbs, 91, 93, 188.
Seville, 143, 191.

Sicily, 59, 93, 116, 126, 139, 149–50, 155.
Siena, 140, 142, 171.
Sigismund, 189, 193–4, 198–9, 200.
Silesia, 83, 122, 142.
Simon de Montfort, 148–9.
Slavs, Slavonic races, 12, 28, 63, 65, 74, 79, 80, 83, 91, 93, 115, 118, 122, 124, 138, 139, 141, 165, 172, 188, 193; see also *Russia, Russians; Serbia, Serbs; Poland, Poles*, &c.
Sluys, 175.
Stephen I of Hungary, St., 84.
Stilicho, 11.
Stockholm, 144.
Strassburg, 60, 154, 186.
Suger of St. Denys, 112, 117.
Swabia, Swabians, 74, 102–3, 116.
Swedes, Sweden, 65, 83–4, 190; see *Scandinavians*.
Swegen Fork-Beard, 84, 90.
Switzerland, Swiss, 156, 168, 170, 177, 188.
Syagrius, 19.
Sylverius, 33.

Tarifa, 175.
Tarik, 48.
Tauler, Johann, 180.
Temple, Templars, Order of, 113, 168–9.
Teutonic Order, Teutonic Knights, 139, 141, 168–9, 193.
Theodora, 31.
Theodore of Tarsus, 46.
Theodoric, 24–5.
Theodosius the Great, 9–10.
Thomas of Aquino, Thomas Aquinas, St., 139, 153, 168.
Thomas Becket, St., 124.
Thorfinn Karlsefne, 89.
Timur, 182, 189, 191, 192.
Togrul Beg, 98.
Toledo, 105.
Toulouse, 134, 140.
Tours, Battle of, 49.
Tribonian, 28, 31.
Troitsa Monastery, 175.
Trondhjem, 83, 90, 107.
Troyes, Treaty of, 200.
Truce of God, 92.